LIKE TO BE A TEABAG

Poems from *Talking Poetry*

Edited by Susan Roberts
Introduced by Nicola Davies
and Simon Rae

I would like to thank Pat Ewing, Gaynor Shutte and Pete Atkin for supporting the *Talking Poetry* project, Lorna Baker and Viv Beeby for helping to put the series into practice, and Sarah Foster and Sue Fry for organising us all.
My thanks also go to the poets who have taken part in the series and contributed to the book, and to the children and schools involved in the poetry workshops.
Finally, a special word of thanks to the two *Talking Poetry* presenters, Nick and Simon.

Susan Roberts

Published by BBC Books,
a division of BBC Enterprises Limited,
Woodlands, 80 Wood Lane, London W12 0TT

First published 1991
Reprinted 1992
Individual poems © individual contributions 1991
Copyright © in this selection BBC Books 1991
Introduction © Susan Roberts 1991
Chapter introductions © Simon Rae and Nicola Davies 1991

ISBN 0 563 36216 2
Illustrations by John Bendall-Brunello

Set in Times Roman by Phoenix Photosetting Ltd, Chatham
Printed and bound by Richard Clay Ltd, St Ives plc, England
Cover printed by Richard Clay Ltd, St Ives plc, England

CONTENTS

INTRODUCTION

I have grown up with a love of poetry, but I know that a lot of people think that if it's poetry, it's got to be boring. Take Molesworth, for example, in *Down with Skool!* 'Peotry is sissy stuff that rhymes. Weedy people say la and fie and swoon when they see a bunch of daffodils.' He could obviously do with a dose of *Talking Poetry*!

This book, which complements the *Talking Poetry* radio series, aims to show how much fun poetry can be, and also to show what poetry can do. With a little imagination it can send Grandad's shed into space, it can float a man in a bowler hat down a canal, it can even produce words from inside a lion. When you begin to investigate the pages of *I'd Like to Be a Teabag*, you'll soon discover that poetry can easily make these things happen – and a lot more.

You'll also find that poetry is more than just 'stuff that rhymes'. Poets use all sorts of different ways to say the things they want to say in a poem and this book is full of them. There are riddles and fables, poems which rhyme, poems which don't rhyme, dialogues, and even recipes – lots of different examples of the ways that patterns of words are used to make poems. When you've had a good look at some of the ideas in the book why don't you think of a shape or an idea and use it to write your own poem?

When I was young I loved writing poetry. I received my first (and last) commission when I was nine – from my mother. She was a primary school teacher at the time and needed a new poem about Hallowe'en to use in the classroom. My poem was not memorable, but I enjoyed the hours I spent on it, and remember proudly handing over the finished version. When I began to plan the new poetry series for Radio 5 which became *Talking Poetry* I was determined that the programme would not only be about listening to poetry but also about writing it.

Every week the radio programme follows a different theme. The first part of the programme features a variety of poems in many different styles, both classic and modern, and by many different poets. The poems are read by children, actors and by the poets themselves. Each of the ten chapters in this book takes one of the ten programme topics of the first series, and you'll find the same rich mix of poetry as in the radio programme.

As well as hearing poems by established poets, Nicola Davies, one of the presenters on *Talking Poetry*, travels around the country eavesdropping on new poems being written. She has been to Liverpool, Cardiff, Belfast, Orkney, Kent and many other places to visit groups of children who have come together on one particular day to write poetry. The results have been spectacular. Here's just one example of a poem written and sent to us by John Williams from Sheffield who is eight years old:

'Night in the Park'

When it's dark and cold
The park is still.
The swing moves gently
Nobody there but the keeper
Or the owl
Hooting!!

Simon Rae is the other presenter on the programme. He's no stranger to writing poetry, as he writes a topical poem each week for a newspaper – the *Weekend Guardian*. I expect all this talk of poetry is beginning to whet your appetite, so I shall hand you immediately over to the presenters. Firstly to Nicola Davies, who has got some tasty poems about food waiting for you, and then to Simon Rae who opens his innings with some train poems which are a real HOOT!

Nicola also gives you her thoughts on Sleep and Dreams, Music, Cats, and the Environment, and Simon shares his musings on Fantasy, The Sea, Conflict, and Night and Dark. When you're reading through the poems in this collection, why don't you jot down some of the thoughts which come into your head and try to turn them into a poem? If you're pleased with the result, send it to:

TALKING POETRY
BBC WHITELADIES ROAD
BRISTOL BS8 2LR

Susan Roberts
Editor, *Talking Poetry*

FOOD

There are some delicious poems in this chapter: poems to make your mouth water. Just peel them off the page and gobble them up.

As an hors-d'oeuvre, to get your imaginative juices flowing, think about what life would be like if we didn't have to eat. Imagine it, no more cooking or washing up, no supermarkets or kitchens, and think of the money we'd save.

> Would the butcher, baker, grocer
> Get our hard-earned dollars? No, Sir!

'If We Didn't Have to Eat' by Nixon Waterman

It may seem like quite an attractive idea, until you think of your favourite food – buttered toast, steak and mushrooms, bananas and custard. And I bet when you imagine those favourite goodies you don't think about the taste alone, because food means more to us than just eating. Everybody has their own private memories and feelings connected with food: images of childhood parties caught in orange jelly like fossil insects in amber, seaside holidays wrapped in the smell of fish and chips.

Now, here is your main course. Think of all the people, places, feelings that food reminds you of. What food would make you long for home if you were far away?

> In London
> every now and then
> I get this craving
> for my mother's food
> I leave art galleries
> in search of plantains
> saltfish/sweet potatoes

'Like a Beacon' by Grace Nichols

What I call 'comfort food' always makes me want to be home – the smell of toast, the steam from a cup of tea. When I'm away from home I always have mushy weetabix for breakfast to remind me of my kids who had that every morning when they were babies!

Now it's time for a dessert, something light and frivolous: a recipe poem! Cookery books would be so much more fun to read if they were written in verse. A line of good poetry can tell you exactly how a recipe is meant to turn out. This description of the amount of onion to add to a salad is so much better than 'half a teaspoon of chopped onion':

> Let onion atoms lurk within the bowl,
> And, scarce suspected, animate the whole.

Convert your favourite recipe to poetry and you'll probably remember it so well that you'll never have to look it up again.

No feast is complete without the cheese course. Even if you hate cheese it, like many foods, is the perfect ingredient for a funny poem. All the different kinds are ripe for rhymes:

> At Christmas the STILTON
> Was spilt on the Wilton,

and a poem can be even funnier if it is made to rhyme at any cost:

> But at New Year the GRUYERE
> It just went straight through yer,
> The CHEDDAR was bedder.

and:

> And if you tried WENSLEYDALE
> You quite *immensely*'d ail.

> 'Say Cheese' by Kit Wright

I rather fancy a poem about different sorts of fruits or sandwich fillings or all the vegetables my father grew in the garden. But that's a different restaurant altogether. Now that you've reached the end of this particular menu you can start your literary meal. Bon appétit!

IF WE DIDN'T HAVE TO EAT

Life would be an easy matter
    If we didn't have to eat.
        If we never had to utter,
            'Won't you pass the bread and butter,
Likewise push along that platter
    Full of meat?'
    Yes, if food were obsolete
    Life would be a jolly treat,
If we didn't – shine or shower,
Old or young, 'bout every hour –
    Have to eat, eat, eat, eat, eat –
    'Twould be jolly if we didn't have to eat.

We could save a lot of money
    If we didn't have to eat.
        Could we cease our busy buying,
        Baking, broiling, brewing, frying,
Life would then be oh, so sunny
    And complete;
    And we wouldn't fear to greet
    Every grocer in the street
If we didn't – man and woman,
Every hungry, helpless human –
    Have to eat, eat, eat, eat, eat –
    We'd save money if we didn't have to eat.

All our worry would be over
    If we didn't have to eat.
        Would the butcher, baker, grocer
        Get our hard-earned dollars? No, Sir!
We would then be right in clover
    Cool and sweet.
    Want and hunger we could cheat,
    And we'd get there with both feet,
If we didn't – poor or wealthy,
Halt or nimble, sick or healthy –
    Have to eat, eat, eat, eat, eat –
    We could get there if we didn't have to eat.

Nixon Waterman

I HATE GREENS

I hate greens!
'They're good for you,' my mother said,
'They'll make the hair curl on your head,
They'll make you grow up big and strong,
That's what your father says.' He's wrong!!

I hate greens.

Peas like bullets, beans like string,
Spinach – not like anything,
Sprouts as hard as bricks and mortar,
Slimy cabbage, slopped in water,

I hate greens.

Swamp them in tomato sauce,
Hide them in your second course,
Though they make you nearly sick,
Close your eyes and gulp them quick,

I hate greens.

Limp lettuce on a lukewarm plate,
Grit in watercress I hate,
Can't bear leeks with dirt inside,
Cauliflower with slugs that died,

I hate greens.

When we go on shopping trips,
Couldn't we have eggs and chips?
Couldn't we have chips and beans?
Don't you know what hunger means?

I HATE GREENS!!!

David King

WHY SHOULDN'T SHE?

My mother loved cooking
but hated washing up
Why shouldn't she?
cooking was an art
she could move her lips to
then the pleasure
feeding the proverbial
multitude (us)
on less than a loaf
and two fishes

Grace Nichols

WHO?

'Who,' asked my mother,
'helped themselves to the *new* loaf?'
   My two friends and I
   looked at her
   and shrugged.

'Who,' questioned my mother,
'broke off the crust?'
   Three pairs of eyes
   stared at the loaf
   lying on the kitchen table.

'Who,' demanded my mother,
'ate the bread?'
   No one replied.
   You could hear
   the kitchen clock. Tick. Tock.

And
even now I can taste it,
crisp, fresh, warm from the bakery,
   and I'd eat it again
   if I could find a loaf
   like that, like that . . .

Wes Magee

THE KING'S BREAKFAST

The King asked
The Queen, and
The Queen asked
The Dairymaid:
'Could we have some butter for
The Royal slice of bread?'
The Queen asked
The Dairymaid,
The Dairymaid
Said, 'Certainly,
I'll go and tell
The cow
Now
Before she goes to bed.'

The Dairymaid
She curtsied,
And went and told
The Alderney:
'Don't forget the butter for
The Royal slice of bread.'
The Alderney
Said sleepily:
'You'd better tell
His Majesty
That many people nowadays
Like marmalade
Instead.'

The Dairymaid
Said, 'Fancy!'
And went to
Her Majesty.
She curtsied to the Queen, and
She turned a little red:
'Excuse me
Your Majesty,
For taking of
The liberty,

But marmalade is tasty, if
It's very
Thickly
Spread.'

The Queen said
'Oh!'
And went to
His Majesty:
'Talking of the butter for
The Royal slice of bread,
Many people
Think that
Marmalade
Is nicer.
Would you like to try a little
Marmalade
Instead?'

The King said,
'Bother!'
And then he said,
'Oh, deary me!'
The King sobbed, 'Oh deary me!'
And went back to bed.
'Nobody,'
He whimpered,
'Could call me
A fussy man;
I *only* want
A little bit
Of butter for
My bread!'

The Queen said
'There, there!'
And went to
The Dairymaid.
The Dairymaid
Said, 'There, there!'
And went to the shed.
The cow said
'There, there!

I didn't really
Mean it;
Here's milk for his porringer
And butter for his bread.'

The Queen took
The butter
And brought it to
His Majesty;
The King said,
'Butter, eh?'
And bounced out of bed.
'Nobody,' he said,
As he kissed her
Tenderly,
'Nobody,' he said,
As he slid down
The banisters,
'Nobody,
My darling,
Could call me
A fussy man –
BUT
I do like a little bit of butter to my bread!'

A. A. Milne

BUTTERFINGERS

When father finished up his toast
he raised his plate for more
so mother buttered some and said,
'Don't drop it on the floor.'
'I'm not a little child!' he cried.
'I never drop my toast,'
then tipped it over on the mat . . .
    and mother laughed the most.

Peggy Dunstan

TOAST

I never had a piece of toast,
Particularly long and wide,
But fell upon the sanded floor
And always on the buttered side.

James Payn

I'D LIKE TO BE A TEABAG

I'd like to be a teabag,
And stay at home all day –
And talk to other teabags
In a teabag sort of way . . .

I'd love to be a teabag,
And lie in a little box –
And never have to wash my face
Or change my dirty socks . . .

I'd like to be a teabag,
An Earl Grey one perhaps,
And doze all day and lie around
With Earl Grey kind of chaps.

I wouldn't have to do a thing,
No homework, jobs or chores –
Comfy in my caddy
Of teabags and their snores.

I wouldn't have to do exams,
I needn't tidy rooms,
Or sweep the floor or feed the cat
Or wash up all the spoons.

I wouldn't have to do a thing,
A life of bliss – you see . . .
Except that once in all my life

I'd make a cup of tea!

Peter Dixon

TO STEW A RUMP-STEAK

Wash it well, and season it hot,
Bind it, and put it in the pot;
Fry three onions, put them to it,
With carrots, turnips, cloves, and suet;
With broth or gravy cover up,
Put in your spoon, and take a sup;
Soft and gentle let it simmer,
Then of port put in a brimmer;
With judgement let the ketchup flow,
Of vinegar a glass bestow;
Simmer again for half an hour,
Serve at six, and then devour.

Anon.

RECIPE FOR SALAD

To make this condiment, your poet begs
The pounded yellow of two hard-boiled eggs,
Two boiled potatoes, passed through kitchen-sieve,
Smoothness and softness to the salad give;
Let onion atoms lurk within the bowl,
And, scarce suspected, animate the whole.
Of mordant mustard add a single spoon,
Distrust the condiment that bites so soon;
But deem it not, thou man of herbs, a fault,
To add a double quantity of salt.
And, lastly, o'er the flavoured compound toss
A magic soup-spoon of anchovy sauce.
Oh, green and glorious! Oh, herbaceous treat!
'Twould tempt the dying anchorite to eat;
Back to the world he'd turn his fleeting soul,
And plunge his fingers in the salad bowl!
Serenely full, the epicure would say,
Fate cannot harm me, I have dined today.

Sydney Smith (19th Century)

RASPBERRY JAM

Take 4 lbs. of fruit.
Use whole clean berries.
Gran's script, the colour
of tea, loops its advice
across a blue-lined pad.

On summer afternoons
we ease ripe berries
from their canes,
heaping them fragrant
into a great glass bowl.

Put in pan. Add 4 lbs.
preserving sugar. Bring
slowly to the boil.
We follow instructions,
stirring in turn.

Keep to a full rolling
boil for five minutes
only. Pot up. The
heaving mass is pocked
with seed, darkens.

Just five minutes. No
more. We let it cool,
pot up into heated jars.
4 + 4 fills 9 pots! Gran's
jam defies the rules.

Moira Andrew

LIKE A BEACON

In London
every now and then
I get this craving
for my mother's food
I leave art galleries
in search of plantains
saltfish/sweet potatoes

I need this link

I need this touch
of home
swinging my bag
like a beacon
against the cold

MANGO

Have a mango
sweet rainwashed sunripe
mango
that the birds themselves
woulda pick
if only they had seen it
a rosy miracle

Here
take it from mih hand

STAR-APPLE

Deepest purple
or pale green white
the star-apple is a sweet fruit
with a sweet star brimming centre
and a turn back skin
that always left me sweetly
sticky mouth

Grace Nichols

GUENIPS

Guenips
hanging in abundant
bunches on the fat knuckled
guenip tree
Guenips
melting like small moons
on my tongue
the succulent green gold
of the fruit kingdom

Grace Nichols

SPAGHETTI! SPAGHETTI!

Spaghetti! spaghetti!
you're wonderful stuff,
I love you, spaghetti,
I can't get enough.
You're covered with sauce
and you're sprinkled with cheese,
spaghetti! spaghetti!
oh, give me some please.

Spaghetti! spaghetti!
piled high in a mound,
you wiggle, you wriggle,
you squiggle around.
There's slurpy spaghetti
all over my plate,
spaghetti! spaghetti!
I think you are great.

Spaghetti! spaghetti!
I love you a lot,
you're slishy, you're sloshy,
delicious and hot.
I gobble you down
oh, I can't get enough,
spaghetti! spaghetti!
you're wonderful stuff.

Jack Prelutsky

SAY CHEESE

At Christmas the STILTON
Was spilt on the Wilton,
The rare CAMEMBERT
Was as fine as can be.
But at New Year the GRUYERE
It just went straight through yer,
The CHEDDAR was bedder
But as for the BRIE,

Aaaaaaaargh! And the PORT SALUT!
Swallow one morsel, you
Kept to your bed
For a week and a day,
And if you tried WENSLEYDALE
You quite *immensely*'d ail,
Hospital-bound
Till they wheeled you away!

No better was EMMENTHAL,
Sour and inclement, all
Cratered and pocked
Like a view of the moon!
And while some are crazy
For creamed BEL PAESE,
Myself, I'd eat forcemeat
Or horsemeat as soon!

The LEICESTER was best o'
The bunch, but the rest o'
Them curled up your stomach.
Though GLOUCESTER (times two)
And jaundiced old CHESHIRE
I'd taste under pressure,
Nothing would get me,
No, nothing would get me,
But nothing would get me
To try DANISH BLUE!

Kit Wright

TRAINS AND STATIONS

All train journeys, even the most day-to-day, are exciting. Of course, the great adventurers who set off on the Patagonian railways, or the great romantic riders of the Orient-Express may sneer at our humdrum journeys into Paddington or Sidcup but I'd rather sit in a train than a car any day.

The train journeys I used to enjoy most were those I took in the summer holidays around Kent to watch the cricket. The trains in those days were the old-fashioned carriage affairs, now gone from most regions – the ones with doors between the rows of bench seats – seats depressed like great spoons, and the luggage racks like string bags.

One of the great pleasures of being on a train is looking out at the countryside speeding past. Whatever you see is suddenly whisked away – 'Each a glimpse and gone for ever!' as Robert Louis Stevenson puts it in 'From a Railway Carriage'.

It's also fun, when the view from the window gets boring, to look at your fellow passengers. What does the man asleep in the corner seat do for a living? Where are the elderly couple opposite going, and why? It might be rude, or at least intrusive, to ask such questions but the imagining mind can always speculate. It's quite clear what the subject of Anthony Thwaite's poem 'The Small Brown Nun' does – or is – but what's going on inside her head?

Stations are obviously part and parcel of railway travel. Modern ones tend to be as characterless and spiritless as airports, but earlier stations display great style and character. Adlestrop in the Cotswolds, immortalised by Edward Thomas, falls into this category. You can still go to Adlestrop station and see the willow-herb and walk along the platform imagining Thomas's train drawing up and nothing happening except all the birds of Oxfordshire and Gloucestershire breaking out in miraculous song.

Michael Rosen inhabits another sort of station in his poem, 'Platform'. Everywhere there's bustle as trains roar through and people climb down from busy commuter trains at the end of a long hard day, and the boy in the poem goes on 'waiting for my mum'. If you wanted to write a poem about the railway, you might find the station you know best a good place to start.

The train that roars through Michael Rosen's station is

the Flying Scotsman. It's impressive, but not quite as impressive as the steam trains that used to run. Those were the trains W. H. Auden knew, and his 'Night Mail' is one of the most famous English poems about trains. It was written back in the 1930s as the sound-track to a film about the Scottish mail train, and Auden actually adapted his poem to fit the film. One of the most striking things about the poem is the way its rhythm appears to mimic the rhythms of the train – the struggle uphill, and then the wonderful freedom of racing away down again once the hill has been conquered.

> Pulling up Beattock, a steady climb:
> The gradient's against her, but she's on time.
>
> Past cotton-grass and moorland boulder,
> Shovelling white steam over her shoulder,
>
> Snorting noisily, she passes
> Silent miles of wind-bent grasses.

One of the most effective images in this poem is that of the jug in the bedroom which gently shakes as the train goes by the sleeping farmhouse. One tiny detail suggests so much: the quietness of the night, the solitude of the farm, and just a hint of tenderness for the people – never mentioned – asleep in the room. And then of course the mood changes and we're running down into the heavily populated areas of Scotland and that marvellous list of all the sorts of letters that the 'Night Mail' is bringing to all the various kinds of people.

'Casey Jones' is another famous railway poem – or, more accurately, song – about a mail train. It's an anonymous ballad, and comes in a long tradition of songs about industrial disasters and the individual deaths of working men. Even though its subject matter is sad, it fairly bustles with energy, the energy of the locomotive going at full steam.

> Casey pulled up Reno Hill,
> Tooted for the crossing with an awful shrill,
> Snakes all knew by the engine's moans
> That the hogger at the throttle was Casey Jones.

SONG OF THE TRAIN

Clickety-clack,
Wheels on the track,
This is the way
They begin the attack:
Click-ety-clack,
Click-ety-clack,
Click-ety, *clack*-ety,
Click-ety
Clack.

Clickety-clack,
Over the crack,
Faster and faster
The song of the track:
Clickety-clack,
Clickety-clack,
Clickety, clackety,
Clackety
Clack.

Riding in front,
Riding in back,
Everyone hears
The song of the track:
Clickety-clack,
Clickety-clack,
Clickety, *clickety*,
Clackety
Clack.

David McCord

FROM A RAILWAY CARRIAGE

Faster than fairies, faster than witches,
Bridges and houses, hedges and ditches;
And charging along like troops in a battle,
All through the meadows the horses and cattle:
All of the sights of the hill and the plain
Fly as thick as driving rain;
And ever again, in the wink of an eye,
Painted stations whistle by.

Here is a child who clambers and scrambles,
All by himself and gathering brambles;
Here is a tramp who stands and gazes;
And there is the green for stringing the daisies!
Here is a cart run away in the road
Lumping along with man and load;
And here is a mill and there is a river:
Each a glimpse and gone for ever!

Robert Louis Stevenson

THE SMALL BROWN NUN

The small brown nun in the corner seat
Smiles out of her wimple and out of her window
Through thick round glasses and through the glass,
And her wimple is white and her habit neat
And whatever she thinks she does not show
As the train jerks on and the low fields pass.

The beer is warm and the train is late
And smoke floats out of the carriage window.
Crosswords are puzzled and papers read,
But the nun, as smooth as a just-washed plate,
Does nothing at all but smile as we go,
As if she listened to something said

Not here, or beyond, or out in the night,
A close old friend with a gentle joke
Telling her something through the window
Inside her head, all neat and right
And snug as the white bound round the yolk
Of a small brown egg in a nest in the snow.

Anthony Thwaite

ON THE TRAIN

When you go on the train
and the line goes past the backs of houses in a town
you can see there's thousands and thousands
of things going on;
someone's washing up,
a baby's crying,
someone's shaving,
someone said, 'Rubbish, I blame the government.'
someone tickled a dog
someone looked out the window
and saw this train
and saw me looking at her
and she thought,
'There's someone looking out the window
looking at me.'

But I'm only someone
looking out the window
looking at someone
looking out the window
looking at someone.

Then it's all gone.

Michael Rosen

ADLESTROP

Yes, I remember Adlestrop –
The name, because one afternoon
Of heat the express-train drew up there
Unwontedly. It was late June.

The steam hissed. Someone cleared his throat.
No one left and no one came
On the bare platform. What I saw
Was Adlestrop – only the name

And willows, willow-herb, and grass,
And meadowsweet, and haycocks dry,
No whit less still and lonely fair
Than the high cloudlets in the sky.

And for that minute a blackbird sang
Close by, and round him, mistier,
Farther and farther, all the birds
Of Oxfordshire and Gloucestershire.

Edward Thomas

PLATFORM

I'm standing on platform one
of Pinner station
at half past four.

Mum comes at ten to five.

When I wait for her
I watch the signals for the express trains change
I watch the lights change
I watch the trains going dark as they
come under the bridge.

I'm waiting for my mum.

I go and stand by the
glass case on the wall
where the Christian Science people
put a Bible for you to read.
It's open and there are bits
of the page marked that you're
supposed to read.
I don't understand it.

I watch the woman in the sweety kiosk
serving people.
Mars Bar, bar of plain chocolate,
packet of chewing gum, Mars Bar, Kit Kat,
barley sugars.

Are you waiting for your mum again?

Yes.

I go and stand on the shiny floor of the waiting room
and look at the big dark benches. There's a boiler in
   there.
They never light it.
Even in winter.

There are big advertisements that I read.

One says:
'Children's shoes have far to go.'
And a boy and girl are walking away
down a long long road to nowhere
with thick woods on both sides of them.
I'm not waiting for a train
I'm waiting for my mum.

At a quarter to
The Flying Scotsman Express Train comes through.
I stand back against the wall.
It's the loudest thing I know.
The station goes dark,
I stop breathing
the coaches move so fast
you can't see the people in them.

At ten to five
Mum's there

The doors open
She'll be in the second carriage,
she always is.

Daylight shines from behind her
so I can't see her face
but I know it's her –
Mum
I know it's her
by her shape
and her bag
and her walk.

Have you been waiting long?
No.
You could have gone home, you know. You've got a
    key.

I like waiting for you.
It's better than being at home on my own.

I suppose it is.

I point to the children
in the big advertisement
'Children's shoes have far to go.'

Where are they going, Mum?

I don't know.

I hold Mum's hand all the way home.

Michael Rosen

THE LATE EXPRESS

There's a train that runs through Hawthorn
3 a.m. or thereabout.
You can hear it hooting sadly,
but no passengers get out.

'That's much too early for a train,'
the station-master said,
'but it's driven by Will Watson
and Willie Watson's dead.'

Poor Willie was a driver
whose record was just fine,
excepting that poor Willie
never learnt to tell the time.

Fathers came home late for dinner,
schoolboys late for their exams,
millionaires had missed on millions,
people changing to the trams.

Oh such fussing and complaining,
even Railways have their pride –
so they sacked poor Willie Watson
and he pined away and died.

Now his ghost reports for duty,
and unrepentant of his crime,
drives a ghost train through here nightly
and it runs to Willie's time.

Barbara Giles

NIGHT MAIL

I

This is the Night Mail crossing the Border,
Bringing the cheque and the postal order,

Letters for the rich, letters for the poor,
The shop at the corner, the girl next door.

Pulling up Beattock, a steady climb:
The gradient's against her, but she's on time.

Past cotton-grass and moorland boulder,
Shovelling white steam over her shoulder,

Snorting noisily, she passes
Silent miles of wind-bent grasses.

Birds turn their heads as she approaches,
Stare from bushes at her blank-faced coaches.

Sheep-dogs cannot turn her course;
They slumber on with paws across.

In the farm she passes no one wakes,
But a jug in a bedroom gently shakes.

II

Dawn freshens. Her climb is done.
Down towards Glasgow she descends,
Towards the steam tugs yelping down a glade of cranes,
Towards the fields of apparatus, the furnaces
Set on the dark plain like gigantic chessmen.
All Scotland waits for her:
In dark glens, beside pale-green lochs,
Men long for news.

III

Letters of thanks, letters from banks,
Letters of joy from girl and boy,
Receipted bills and invitations
To inspect new stock or to visit relations,
And applications for situations,
And timid lovers' declarations,
And gossip, gossip from all the nations,
News circumstantial, news financial,
Letters with holiday snaps to enlarge in,
Letters with faces scrawled on the margin,
Letters from uncles, cousins and aunts,
Letters to Scotland from the South of France,
Letters of condolence to Highlands and Lowlands,
Written on paper of every hue,
The pink, the violet, the white and the blue,
The chatty, the catty, the boring, the adoring,
The cold and official and the heart's outpouring,
Clever, stupid, short and long,
The typed and the printed and the spelt all wrong.

IV

Thousands are still asleep,
Dreaming of terrifying monsters
Or a friendly tea beside the band in Cranston's
    or Crawford's:
Asleep in working Glasgow, asleep in well-set
    Edinburgh
Asleep in granite Aberdeen,
They continue their dreams,
But shall wake soon and hope for letters,
And none will hear the postman's knock
Without a quickening of the heart.
For who can bear to feel himself forgotten?

W. H. Auden

33

CASEY JONES

Come all you rounders if you want to hear
The story of a brave engineer;
Casey Jones was the hogger's name,
On a big eight-wheeler, boys, he won his fame.
Caller called Casey at half-past four,
He kissed his wife at the station door,
Mounted to the cabin with orders in his hand,
And took his farewell trip to the promised land.

    Casey Jones, he mounted to the cabin,
    Casey Jones, with his orders in his hand!
    Casey Jones, he mounted to the cabin,
    Took his farewell trip into the promised land.

'Put in your water and shovel in your coal,
Put your head out the window, watch the drivers roll,
I'll run her till she leaves the rail,
'Cause we're eight hours late with the Western Mail!'
He looked at his watch and his watch was slow,
Looked at the water and the water was low,
Turned to his fireboy and said,
'We'll get to 'Frisco, but we'll all be dead!'

    Casey Jones, he mounted to the cabin,
    Casey Jones, with his orders in his hand!
    Casey Jones, he mounted to the cabin,
    Took his farewell trip into the promised land.

Casey pulled up Reno Hill,
Tooted for the crossing with an awful shrill,
Snakes all knew by the engine's moans
That the hogger at the throttle was Casey Jones.
He pulled up short two miles from the place,
Number Four stared him right in the face,
Turned to his fireboy, said, 'You'd better jump,
'Cause there's two locomotives that's going to bump.'

Casey Jones, he mounted to the cabin,
Casey Jones, with his orders in his hand!
Casey Jones, he mounted to the cabin,
Took his farewell trip into the promised land.

Casey said, just before he died,
'There's two more roads I'd like to ride.'
Fireboy said, 'What can they be?'
'The Rio Grande and the Old S.P.'
Mrs. Jones sat on her bed a-sighing,
Got a pink that Casey was dying.
Said, 'Go to bed, children; hush your crying,
'Cause you'll get another papa on the Salt Lake line.'

Casey Jones! Got another papa!
Casey Jones, on the Salt Lake Line!
Casey Jones! Got another papa!
Got another papa on the Salt Lake Line!

Anon.

SLEEP AND DREAMS

Shivering, my feet frozen on the icy tiles of a winter kitchen floor, all I want to do is go back to bed. All over the country on winter mornings people are waiting at draughty bus stops, brushing their teeth in arctic bathrooms, sleepily pulling on clothes, and all of them dreaming of one thing: bed. Beautiful warm, cosy, comforting, safe, snuggly . . . bed.

> Oh, the snuggly bits
> Where the pillow fits
>
> Oh, the beautiful heat
> Stored under the sheet
>
> 'Ned' by Eleanor Farjeon

But however hard it is for all of those people to get up in the morning, an awful lot of them will have even more trouble doing the reverse at the other end of the day. Children who found their bed far too good to get out of will be fighting hard not to get back in it at night. I was terrified of bedtime when I was little, convinced that every shadow held a nameless 'THING'. I had to have certain combinations of doors shut and lights left on before I could even lie down. And as for getting to sleep – impossible!

> They said,
> 'If you can't get to sleep
>   try counting sheep.'
> I tried.
> It didn't work.
>
> 'Counting Sheep' by Wes Magee

It never worked for me. My sheep always turned into monsters that scared me even more wide awake. I wish I'd known this brilliant monster cure when I was young.

> Do little sleeping monsters scream
> Who dream
> Of meeting me?
>
> 'I Often Meet a Monster' by Max Fatchen

I wonder if sheep try counting humans when they need a snooze? After you've counted sheep, monsters or people you finally make that tricky change from an awake person into a sleeping person. You enter the world of dreams where anything can happen. Events and people from your real life and from imagination are jumbled and mixed as your brain does its night-time filing. My father called this dream world 'The Land of Nod' but I never really understood who Nod was until my mother read me the poem about him by Walter de la Mare:

> Softly along the road of evening,
>   In a twilight dim with rose,
> Wrinkled with age, and drenched with dew,
>   Old Nod, the shepherd, goes.

I hadn't heard that poem for over twenty years when it turned up for *Talking Poetry* and I could still remember the picture of Nod that the words made.

SWEET DREAMS

I wonder as into bed I creep
What it feels like to fall asleep.
I've told myself stories, I've counted sheep,
But I'm always asleep when I fall asleep.
Tonight my eyes I will open keep,
And I'll stay awake till I fall asleep,
Then I'll know what it feels like to fall asleep,
Asleep,
Asleeep,
Asleeeep . . .

Ogden Nash

I'VE TAKEN TO MY BED

I've taken to my bed
(And my bed has taken to me)
We're getting married in the spring
How happy we shall be

We'll raise lots of little bunks
A sleeping-bag or two
Take my advice: find a bed that's nice
Lie down and say: 'I love you.'

Roger McGough

I LIKE TO STAY UP

I like to stay up
and listen
when big people talking
jumbie stories

I does feel
so tingly and excited
inside me

But when my mother say
'Girl, time for bed'

Then is when
I does feel a dread

Then is when
I does cover up
from me feet to me head

Then is when
I does wish I didn't listen
to no stupid jumbie story

Then is when
I does wish I did read
me book instead

Grace Nichols

Jumbie – Guyanese word for ghost

NED

It's a singular thing that Ned
Can't be got out of bed.
   When the sun comes round
   He is sleeping sound
With blankets over his head.
   They tell him to shunt,
   And he gives a grunt,
And burrows a little deeper –
   He's a trial to them
   At eight a.m.,
When Ned is a non-stop sleeper.
   Oh, the snuggly bits
   Where the pillow fits
   Into his cheeks and neck!
   Oh, the beautiful heat
   Stored under the sheet
Which the breakfast-bell will wreck!
Oo, the noozly-oozly feel
He feels from head to heel,
   When to get out of bed
   Is worse to Ned
Than missing his morning meal!
        But
It's a singular thing that Ned,
   After the sun is dead
   And the moon's come round,
   Is not to be found,
   And can't be got into bed!

Eleanor Farjeon

TOO HOT TO SLEEP

He was sleeping when bear
came down from the mountain
by the water trap
after cleaning the screen
of branches and gravel

He fell asleep, a hot June morning
above Wapta Lake, the Kicking Horse Pass
When Muskwa came down without a sound
And snuffed at his jeans

Who's this asleep on my mountain?

It's my friend Birnie asleep I said
(in my head)
I didn't hear you coming bear
I was dozing, I looked up
and there you were

You never know said Bear
just where the wind will lead me
when I'll be around
or what beat I'm hunting on

and sniffed at Birnie's collar
at his ear, which he licked tentatively
causing Birnie to moan softly

Nothing doing here he said, nothing doing

'We were just going bear,' I said quietly
edging backwards

Don't move too quickly will you, said Bear
when you move, or better still
don't move at all

Are you here often, are you coming again?
he asked, flipping over a stone
licking delicately the underside
'No,' I said, good he said, that's good.

I just came down from the pass
the wind blowing up my nose
to see who was sleeping on my mountain
he said, and sniffed at Birnie's armpit
Whoosh   whoosh he snorted

and turned away, clattered down the creek
popping his teeth, his hackles up
Went out of sight
around the shoulder of Mount Hector

as Birnie woke rubbing his eyes
'Too hot to sleep he said.' Yeah.

Sid Marty

CUDDLE DOON

The bairnies cuddle doon at nicht
  Wi' muckle faught an' din;
'Oh try and sleep, ye waukrife rogues,
  Your faither's comin' in.'
They never heed a word I speak;
  I try to gie a froon,
But aye I hap them up an' cry,
  'Oh, bairnies, cuddle doon.'

Wee Jamie wi' the curly heid –
  He aye sleeps next the wa',
Bangs up an' cries, 'I want a piece' –
  The rascal starts them a'.
I rin an' fetch them pieces, drinks,
  They stop awee the soun',
Then draw the blankets up an' cry,
  'Noo, weanies, cuddle doon.'

But ere five minutes gan, wee Rab
  Cries out, frae 'neath the claes,
'Mither, mak' Tam gie ower at ance,
  He's kittlin' wi' his taes.'

The mischief's in that Tam for tricks,
   He'd bother half the toon;
But aye I hap them up an' cry,
   'Oh, bairnies, cuddle doon.'

At length they hear their faither's fit,
   An', as he steeks the door,
They turn their faces to the wa',
   While Tam pretends to snore.
'Hae a' the weans been gude?' he asks,
   As he pits aff his shoon;
'The bairnies, John, are in their beds,
   An' lang since cuddled doon.'

An' just afore we bed oorsel's,
   We look at our wee lambs,
Tam has his airm roun' wee Rab's neck,
   And Rab his airm round Tam's.
I lift wee Jamie up the bed,
   An' as I straik each croon,
I whisper, till my heart fills up,
   'Oh, bairnies, cuddle doon.'

The bairnies cuddle doon at nicht
   Wi' mirth that's dear to me;
But soon the big warl's cark an' care
   Will quaten doon their glee.
Yet, come what will to ilka ane,
   May He who rules aboon
Aye whisper, though their pows be bald,
   'Oh, bairnies, cuddle doon.'

Alexander Anderson

PILLOW TALK

Last night I heard my pillow talk
What amazing things it said
About the fun that pillows have
Before it's time for bed

The bedroom is their playground
A magical place to be
(Not a room for peace and quiet
Like it is for you and me)

They divebomb off the wardrobe
Do backflips off the chair
Use the mattress as a trampoline
Turn somersaults in the air

It's Leapfrog then Pass the Slipper
Handstands and cartwheels all round
Wrestling and swinging on curtains
And all with hardly a sound

But by and by the feathers fly
And they get out of puff
So with scarves and ties they bind their eyes
For a game of Blind Man's Buff

They tiptoe out on the landing
Although it's a dangerous place
(If granny met one on the stairs
Imagine the look on her face!)

It's pillows who open cupboard drawers
To mess and rummage about
(And *you* end up by getting blamed
For something *they* left out)

I'd quite fancy being a pillow
Playing games and lying in bed
If I didn't have to spend each night
Under your big snoring head!

Roger McGough

45

STOPPING BY WOODS
ON A SNOWY EVENING

Whose woods these are I think I know.
His house is in the village, though;
He will not see me stopping here
To watch his woods fill up with snow.

My little horse must think it queer
To stop without a farmhouse near
Between the woods and frozen lake
The darkest evening of the year.

He gives his harness bells a shake
To ask if there is some mistake.
The only other sound's the sweep
Of easy wind and downy flake.

The woods are lovely, dark, and deep,
But I have promises to keep,
And miles to go before I sleep,
And miles to go before I sleep.

Robert Frost

NOD

Softly along the road of evening,
    In a twilight dim with rose,
Wrinkled with age, and drenched with dew,
    Old Nod, the shepherd, goes.

His drowsy flock streams on before him,
    Their fleeces charged with gold,
To where the sun's last beam leans low
    On Nod the shepherd's fold.

The hedge is quick and green with briar,
  From their sand the conies creep;
And all the birds that fly in heaven
  Flock singing home to sleep.

His lambs outnumber a noon's roses,
  Yet, when night's shadows fall,
His blind old sheep-dog, Slumber-soon,
  Misses not one of all.

His are the quiet steeps of dreamland,
  The waters of no-more-pain;
His ram's bell rings 'neath an arch of stars,
  'Rest, rest, and rest again.'

Walter de la Mare

COUNTING SHEEP

They said,
'If you can't get to sleep
  try counting sheep.'
I tried.
It didn't work.

They said,
'Still awake! Count rabbits, dogs,
  or leaping frogs!'
I tried.
It didn't work.

They said,
'It's *very* late! Count rats,
  or red-eyed bats!'
I tried.
It didn't work.

They said,
'Stop counting stupid sheep!
  EYES CLOSED! DON'T PEEP!'
I tried.
And fell asleep.

Wes Magee

PILLOW FIGHT

As soon as my head
Hit the pillow
The pillow hit my head back

Hammering tongues
They were at it
Hammer and tongs

I sat up
And tried to separate them
But in vain

As soon as my head
Hit the pillow again
The pillow fought back

So I counted slowly
Up to ten
Then everything went black.

Roger McGough

I OFTEN MEET A MONSTER

I often meet a monster
While deep asleep at night;
And I confess to some distress.
It gives me quite a fright.
But then again I wonder.
I have this thought, you see.
Do little sleeping monsters scream
Who dream
Of meeting me?

Max Fatchen

COLOUR OF MY DREAMS

I'm a really rotten reader
the worst in all the class,
the sort of rotten reader
that makes you want to laugh.

I'm last in all the readin' tests,
my score's not on the page
and when I read to teacher
she gets in such a rage.

She says I cannot form my words
she says I can't build up
and that I don't know phonics
– and don't know a c-a-t from k-u-p.

They say that I'm dyxlectic
(that's a word they've just found out)
. . . but when I get some plasticine
I know what that's about.

I make these scary monsters
I draw these secret lands
and get my hair all sticky
and paint on all me hands.

I make these super models,
I build these smashing towers
that reach up to the ceiling
– and take me hours and hours.

I paint these lovely pictures
in thick green drippy paint
that gets all on the carpet –
and makes the cleaners faint.

I build great magic forests
weave bushes out of string
and paint pink panderellos
and birds that really sing.

I play my world of real believe
I play it every day
and teachers stand and watch me
but don't know what to say

They give me diagnostic tests,
they try out reading schemes,
but none of them will ever know
the colour of my dreams.

Peter Dixon

I WAKE UP

I wake up
I am not me
I am bodyless
I am weightless
I am legless
I am armless
I am in the sea of my mind
I am in the middle of my brain
I am afloat in a sea of nothing

It lasts for one flicker
of one eyelash

and then
once again
I am my full heaviness
I am my full headedness
I am my full bodyness
Here.
Hallo.

Michael Rosen

THE POET INSPIRED

7-30 on a pristine June morning
Sitting up in bed, pen in hand
The poet is ready to compose
The first poem of the day.

A subject? He thinks around
For something to write about.
Sheep. Counting sheep! Yes,
That would be a worthy challenge.

A poem about counting sheep.
Counting sheep. 1 – 2 – 3. Counting
Sheep – 4 –5. Sheep. Count
6 – Sheep. Sheee . . . z – z – z.

Roger McGough

THE SEA

I sometimes think I could look at the sea all day, even when it's calm. Without a breath of wind, or the least pull of the tide, it's always alive, always rippling with motion, and if the sun's shining it's like looking out over a great tray of diamonds. And, of course, when it's the least bit rough, it's riveting – those great waves rolling in, suddenly surging up and over the rocks; the crash of spray, the wait for the next one, which is never the same.

And then there are the people and boats who go to sea, the things people do on and under the sea, and the creatures and things that inhabit the sea. It's a whole world; an alternative world to that of dry land. Even though I'm not a sea-going person I find that world captivating. So too have the poets. I doubt whether there's a more evocative poem in the language than John Masefield's 'Sea-Fever':

I must down to the seas again, to the lonely sea and the sky,
And all I ask is a tall ship and a star to steer her by,

unless, of course, it's his other great sea poem, 'Cargoes':

Quinquireme of Nineveh from distant Ophir
Rowing home to haven in sunny Palestine,
With a cargo of ivory,
And apes and peacocks,
Sandalwood, cedarwood, and sweet white wine.

But then, Masefield was sent away to sea as a boy and had crossed the Atlantic a couple of times before he was twenty. The sea was in his blood.

It's also in Charles Causley's blood. As a Cornishman, he comes from one of the parts of Britain most closely associated with the sea in all its wide variety of moods; and he also served as a sailor in the Second World War. 'Dan Dory' is an account of a meeting with the ghost of a fellow sailor lost on active service, while 'Tell Me, Tell Me, Sarah Jane' demonstrates the enthralling power of the sea:

Mother I hear the water
    Beneath the headland pinned,
And I can see the sea-gull
    Sliding down the wind.
I taste the salt upon my tongue
    As sweet as sweet can be.

Tell me, my dear, whose voice you hear?

It is the sea, the sea.

But what of the creatures that inhabit the sea? One of the most terrifying films I have ever seen is *Jaws*, about a battle with a great white shark of staggering size and strength. 'He has a very dangerous bite', is something of an under-statement on the part of Lord Alfred Douglas. But there's no denying that, along with the horror of that great cavern of ferocious teeth, there's a fascination with perhaps the most efficient killing-machine in the animal kingdom.

Far more peaceable is the whale (though that, sadly, has not saved it from the most savage killing-machine of all – man). Whales are not only enormous; they're enormously intelligent. They live peacefully together, communicating in the most extraordinary sonic music that booms and reverberates around the waters where they live. The story of Jonah and the Whale is among the best known from the Old Testament and, like so many popular Bible stories, it has been re-told, in pictures, poems, and stories, hundreds of times. Here it's Gareth Owen's turn:

Well, to start with
It was dark
So dark
You couldn't see
Your hand in front of your face . . .

But it's a game anyone can play. Why don't you try? What would it be like inside a whale? And how, if you'd been inside one, would you get your friends to imagine it?

The inside of a whale is far removed from the family day at the beach with bucket and spade and – the one ingre-dient that there always seems to be too much of – sand. It gets everywhere, and sticks with you for days, as John Foster reminds us in his poem:

Sand in your fingernails
Sand between your toes
Sand in your earholes
Sand up your nose!

And when all's said and done, if you're a land-lubber like
me, you'll settle for a deckchair and a nice patch of beach,
with the sea a friendly presence beyond the donkey rides
and the ice-cream vans.

SAND

Sand in your fingernails
Sand between your toes
Sand in your earholes
Sand up your nose!

Sand in your sandwiches
Sand on your bananas
Sand in your bed at night
Sand in your pyjamas!

Sand in your sandals
Sand in your hair
Sand in your trousers
Sand everywhere!

John Foster

SEA TALK

Inside the little harbour, on the tide
That washes stones where weedy limpets cling,
I thought I heard where sleeping rowboats ride,
The little fishes' tiny whispering.

I thought I heard, beside the wooden pier,
The starfish heave a long and salty sigh
And murmur in the mussel's shelly ear,
Its longing for a bright and wider sky.

I thought I heard the underwater shouts
Of gleeful creatures . . . moans and barks and squeals,
The dolphins thrusting long and smiling snouts
And gossiping to sleek and agile seals. . . .

The noises from the restless waves and spray
Of armoured crabs that guard their rocky spots,
The sound of white sea horses at their play
Or lobsters' prayers within their captive pots.

I wish I knew that such a thing could be –
To know the songs of moving fin and scales,
The liquid language of the living sea
And hear the gentle voices of the whales.

Max Fatchen

ANCHORED

Our anchor's too big for our ship,
So we're sittin' here tryin' to think.
If we leave it behind we'll be lost.
If we haul it on board, we will sink.
If we sit and keep talkin' about it,
It will soon be too late for our trip.
It sure can be rough on a sailor
When the anchor's too big for the ship.

Shel Silverstein

UNCLE RODERICK

His drifter swung in the night
from a mile of nets
between the Shiants and Harris.

My boy's eyes watched
the lights of the fishing fleet – fireflies
on the green field of the sea.

In the fo'c'sle he gave me a bowl
of tea, black, strong and bitter,
and a biscuit you hammered
in bits like a plate.

The fiery curtain came up
from the blackness, comma'd with corpses.

Round Rhu nan Cuideagan
he steered for home, a boy's god
in seaboots. He found his anchorage
as a bird its nest.

In the kitchen he dropped
his oilskins where he stood.

He was strong as the red bull.
He moved like a dancer.
He was a cran of songs.

Norman MacCaig

cran: a measure of fresh herrings (about 750 fish)

DAN DORY

Today I saw Dan Dory
Walking out of the sea.
'Did you tell the world my story?'
Dan said to me.

Salt glittered on his breast, his fingers.
Drops of gold fell from his hair.
The look in his eye was sapphire-bright
As he stood there.

'Your head is white,' said Dan Dory.
'Trenched your face, your hand.
And why do you walk to greet me
So slowly across the sand?'

'I watched you held, Dan Dory,
In ocean fast.
Thirty, no, forty years ago
I saw you last.

'And now I see you older
By not a second's stroke.
Than when the sun raged overhead
And the sea was flame, was smoke.'

'Did you tell the world my story?'
I heard him say.
'And for the unwisdom of the old
Do the young still pay?'

'Still spins the water and the land,'
I said, 'as yesterday' –
And leaned to take his hand. But he
Had vanished away.

Charles Causley

THE SHARK

A treacherous monster is the Shark
He never makes the least remark.

And when he sees you on the sand,
He doesn't seem to want to land.

He watches you take off your clothes,
And not the least excitement shows.

His eyes do not grow bright or roll,
He has astounding self-control.

He waits till you are quite undrest,
And seems to take no interest.

And when towards the sea you leap,
He looks as if he were asleep.

But when you once get in his range,
His whole demeanour seems to change.

He throws his body right about,
And his true character comes out.

It's no usc crying or appealing,
He seems to lose all decent feeling.

After this warning you will wish
To keep clear of this treacherous fish.

His back is black, his stomach white,
He has a very dangerous bite.

Lord Alfred Douglas

JONAH AND THE WHALE

Well, to start with
It was dark
So dark
You couldn't see
Your hand in front of your face;
And huge
Huge as an acre of farmland.
How do I know?
Well, I paced it out
Length and breadth
That's how.
And if you was to shout
You'd hear your own voice resound,
Bouncing along the ridges of its stomach,
Like when you call out
Under a bridge
Or in an empty hall.
Hear anything?
No not much,
Only the normal
Kind of sounds
You'd expect to hear
Inside a whale's stomach;
The sea swishing far away,
Food gurgling, the wind
And suchlike sounds;
Then there was me screaming for help,
But who'd be likely to hear,
Us being miles from
Any shipping lines
And anyway
Supposing someone did hear,
Who'd think of looking inside a whale?
That's not the sort of thing
That people do.
Smell?
I'll say there was a smell.
And cold. The wind blew in
Something terrible from the South
Each time he opened his mouth
Or took a swallow of some tit bit.

The only way I found
To keep alive at all
Was to wrap my arms
Tight round myself
And race from wall to wall.
Damp? You can say that again;
When the ocean came sluicing in
I had to climb his ribs
To save myself from drowning.
Fibs? You think I'm telling you fibs,
I haven't told the half of it.
Brother
I'm only giving a modest account
Of what these two eyes have seen
And that's the truth on it.
Here, one thing I'll say
Before I'm done –
Catch me eating fish
From now on.

Gareth Owen

CARGOES

Quinquireme of Nineveh from distant Ophir
Rowing home to haven in sunny Palestine,
With a cargo of ivory,
And apes and peacocks,
Sandalwood, cedarwood, and sweet white wine.

Stately Spanish galleon coming from the Isthmus,
Dipping through the Tropics by the palm-green shores,
With a cargo of diamonds,
Emeralds, amethysts,
Topazes, and cinnamon, and gold moidores.

Dirty British coaster with a salt-caked smoke stack
Butting through the Channel in the mad March days,
With a cargo of Tyne coal,
Road-rail, pig-lead,
Firewood, iron-ware, and cheap tin trays.

John Masefield

SEA-FEVER

I must down to the seas again, to the lonely sea and the
  sky,
And all I ask is a tall ship and a star to steer her by,
And the wheel's kick and the wind's song and the white
  sail's shaking,
And a grey mist on the sea's face and a grey dawn
  breaking.

I must down to the seas again, for the call of the running
  tide
Is a wild call and a clear call that may not be denied;
And all I ask is a windy day with the white clouds flying,
And the flung spray and the blown spume, and the
  sea-gulls crying.

I must down to the seas again, to the vagrant gypsy life,
To the gull's way and the whale's way where the wind's
  like a whetted knife;
And all I ask is a merry yarn from a laughing fellow-
  rover,
And quiet sleep and a sweet dream when the long trick's
  over.

John Masefield

ME – PIRATE

If ever I go to sea,
I think I'll be a pirate:
I'll have a treasure-ship in tow,
And a man-of-war to fire at.

With a cutlass at my belt,
And a pistol in my hand,
I'll nail my Crossbones to the mast
And sail for a foreign land.

And when we reach that shore,
We'll beat our battle-drum
And fire a salute of fifteen guns
To tell them we have come.

We'll fight them all day long;
We'll seize their chests of gold,
Their diamonds, coins and necklaces,
And stuff them in our hold.

A year and a day at home,
Then off on the waves again –
Lord of the Caribbean Seas
King of the Spanish Main!

Clive Sansom

A SMUGGLERS' SONG

If you wake at midnight, and hear a horse's feet,
Don't go drawing back the blind, or looking in the
    street,
Them that asks no questions isn't told a lie.
Watch the wall, my darling, while the Gentlemen go by!
       Five-and-twenty ponies,
       Trotting through the dark –
       Brandy for the Parson,
       'Baccy for the Clerk;
       Laces for a lady; letters for a spy,
And watch the wall, my darling, while the Gentlemen go
    by!

Running round the woodlump if you chance to find
Little barrels, roped and tarred, all full of brandy-wine;
Don't you shout to come and look, nor take 'em for your
    play;
Put the brushwood back again, – and they'll be gone
    next day!

If you see the stable-door setting open wide;
If you see a tired horse lying down inside;
If your mother mends a coat cut about and tore;
If the lining's wet and warm – don't you ask no more!

If you meet King George's men, dressed in blue and red,
You be careful what you say, and mindful what is said.
If they call you 'pretty maid,' and chuck you 'neath the
    chin,
Don't you tell where no one is, nor yet where no one's
    been!

Knocks and footsteps round the house – whistles after
    dark –
You've no call for running out till the house-dogs bark.
Trusty's here, and Pincher's here, and see how dumb
    they lie –
They don't fret to follow when the Gentlemen go by!

If you do as you've been told, likely there's a chance
You'll be given a dainty doll, all the way from France,
With a cap of Valenciennes, and a velvet hood –
A present from the Gentlemen, along o' being good!
            Five-and-twenty ponies,
            Trotting through the dark –
            Brandy for the Parson,
            'Baccy for the Clerk.
Them that asks no questions isn't told a lie –
Watch the wall, my darling, while the Gentlemen go by!

Rudyard Kipling

TELL ME, TELL ME,
SARAH JANE

Tell me, tell me, Sarah Jane,
    Tell me, dearest daughter,
Why are you holding in your hand
    A thimbleful of water?
Why do you hold it to your eye
    And gaze both late and soon
From early morning light until
    The rising of the moon?

Mother, I hear the mermaids cry,
    I hear the mermen sing,
And I can see the sailing-ships
    All made of sticks and string.
And I can see the jumping fish,
    The whales that fall and rise
And swim about the waterspout
    That swarms up to the skies.

Tell me, tell me, Sarah Jane,
    Tell your darling mother,
Why do you walk beside the tide
    As though you loved none other?
Why do you listen to a shell
    And watch the billows curl,
And throw away your diamond ring
    And wear instead the pearl?

Mother I hear the water
    Beneath the headland pinned,
And I can see the sea-gull
    Sliding down the wind.
I taste the salt upon my tongue
    As sweet as sweet can be.

Tell me, my dear, whose voice you hear?

It is the sea, the sea.

                    Charles Causley

MUSIC

Music fascinates me. Why is it that we should find certain collections of sounds beautiful? Why should they make us want to laugh, cry, sing, dance, remember? I'm too much under the influence of music to be able to analyse it. It can change my mood completely and I can't bear to be without it for very long. I'm no musician, so the whole business of music-making fascinates me too – the gleam and creak of the instruments, the way the musicians touch them with such gentle familiarity. And then the way all the different shapes and sizes of instruments and musicians, and all the squeaks, squawks, whinings, pluckings and bangings, suddenly become music.

> 'Zoomba-zoom,' said the bass,
> 'Pickle-pee,' said the fife,
> 'Pump-a-rum,' said the drum,
> 'Tootle-too,' said the flute,
> 'Deed-a-reedle,' said the fiddle,
> For the fiddles and the flutes were
> the finest in the land.

That's how James Reeves expresses the making of music in his poem 'The Ceremonial Band'. They are very simple, almost comical, words but they capture the exhilaration of all that glorious, harmonious noise. In fact, the poem actually begins to sound like the band. In 'Mek Drum Talk, Man' James Berry makes the words sound like drums to make the drums talk like words. It's a wonderful example of the way words work in two ways in a poem – what they mean and what they sound like.

> Slap the drum. Elbow drum. Thump drum.
> Mek drum sey to be hit is fun.
> Wake up skin. Wake up skin
> with it broom bu-doom it hidin.

You really have to read this one out loud and feel its rhythm to get the full effect of the Caribbean Carnival.

Writing about music gives a poet a huge variety of subjects, from heavy metal to Mozart, punk rockers to promenaders, tears to laughter, waltzes to break-dancing. And, of course, a poet can be the dancer . . .

. . . when I dance
I'm costumed in a rainbow mood,
I'm OK at any angle,

'When I Dance' by James Berry

. . . or the musician . . .

When I play on my fiddle in Dooney
Folk dance like the wave of the sea;

'The Fiddler of Dooney' by W. B. Yeats

. . . or the instrument, or the conductor, or the audience, or the singer, or even the vibrating notes of music as they spring to life in the air.

EMBRIONIC MEGA-STARS

We can play reggae music, funk and skiffle too,
We prefer heavy metal but the classics sometimes do.
We're keen on Tamla-Motown, folk and soul,
But most of all, what we like
Is basic rock and roll.
We can play the monochord, the heptachord and flute,
We're OK on the saxophone and think the glockenspiel
　　is cute,
We really love the tuba, the balalaika and guitar
And our duets on the clavichord are bound to take us
　　far.
We think castanets are smashing, harmonicas are fun,
And with the ocarina have only just begun.
We've mastered synthesizers, bassoons and violins
As well as hurdy-gurdies, pan-pipes and mandolins.
The tom-tom and the tabor, the trumpet and the drum
We learnt to play in between the tintinnabulum.
We want to form a pop group
And will when we're eleven,
But at the moment Tracey's eight
And I am only seven.

Brian Patten

JAZZ-MAN

　　　Crash and
　　　　　　CLANG!
　　　Bash and
　　　　　　BANG!

And up in the road the Jazz-Man sprang!
The One-Man-Jazz-Band playing in the street,
Drums with his Elbows, Cymbals with his Feet,
Pipes with his Mouth, Accordian with his Hand,
Playing all his Instruments to Beat the Band!

　　　TOOT and
　　　　　　Tingle!
　　　HOOT and
　　　　　　Jingle!

Oh, what a Clatter! How the tunes all mingle!
Twenty Children couldn't make as much Noise as
The Howling Pandemonium of the One-Man-Jazz!

Eleanor Farjeon

MOON MUSIC

The pianos on the moon are so long
The pianist's hand must be fifteen fingers strong.

The violins on the moon are so violent
They have to be sunk in deep wells, and then they only
    seem to be silent.

The bassoons on the moon blow no notes
But huge blue loons that flap slowly away with
    undulating throats.

Now harmonicas on the moon are humorous,
The tunes produce German Measles, but the speckles
    more numerous.

Of a trumpet on the moon you can never hear enough
Because it puffs the trumpeter up like a balloon and he
    floats off.

Double basses on the moon are a risk all right,
At the first note enormous black hands appear and carry
    away everything in sight.

Even a triangle on the moon is risky,
One ping – and there's your head a half bottle of Irish
    whisky.

In the same way, be careful with the flute –
Because wherever he is, your father will find himself
    converted into a disgusting old boot.

On the whole it's best to stick to the moon's drums.
Whatever damage they do is so far off in space the news
    never comes.

Ted Hughes

MEK DRUM TALK, MAN

for Caribbean Independence

Budoom-a budoom-a budoom-a ba-dap.
A-dudu-wum a-dudu-wum dudu-wum a-dudu-wum.
Wake skin up. Wake skin.
Slap it up. Slap skin.
Man, slap up drum.
Use yu hundred han them.
Domination get drop.
Some doors get open up.

    Lawks O, slap the drum, slap it Buddy.
    Slap it like yu a mad mad somody –
    budoom-a budoom-a budoom-a ba-dap,
    budoom-a budoom-a budoom-a ba-dap.
    A-dudu-wum a-dudu-wum dudu-wum a-dudu-wum.
    Budoom a dudu-wum. Budoom-a dudu-wum. Bru-dum.

Let out lost ancestor voice.
Let out of skin all pain and vice.
Tell the worl that the king is dead –
forbidden people gettn wed.
Tell towns new words comin fo print –
knowledge looked-fo whe palms they skint.
Get soun like them a talkin gong,
mek them happy jus a-galang.

Get the soun, get the soun, get it Buddy.
Wake up gong and family.
Every soun is head with a hum
of deep-deep voice of drum –
tru the windows, tru the trees,
tru the markets, tru the streets.

Lawks O, slap the drum, slap it Buddy.
Slap it like yu a mad mad somody –
budoom-a budoom-a budoom-a ba-dap,
budoom-a budoom-a budoom-a ba-dap.
A-dudu-wum a-dudu-wum dudu-wum a-dudu-wum.
Budoom-a dudu-wum. Budoom-a dudu-wum. Bru-dum.

Slap the drum. Elbow drum. Thump drum.
Mek drum sey to be hit is fun.
Wake up skin. Wake up skin
with it broom bu-doom it hidin.
People cry – start a new cycle!
Widen money circle!
Get out every hiddn moan.
Let loose all skin-hiddn groan.

Show off the pulse of big bright sun.
Sen good news to village and town.
Tell the people a child is born,
tell them about a sweet new dawn.
Bring street drummin in the house –
see sleepers get aroused.
Wake the people out-a they trance.
Tell people come dance.

Lawks O, slap the drum, slap it Buddy.
Slap it like yu a mad mad somody –
budoom-a budoom-a budoom-a ba-dap,
budoom-a budoom-a budoom-a ba-dap.
A-dudu-wum a-dudu-wum dudu-wum a-dudu-wum.
Budoom-a dudu-wum. Budoom-a dudu-wum. Bru-dum.

James Berry

a-galang: going along   somody: somebody

DANCING IN THE DUST

Croesus was as rich as sin.
Cyrus and his son
Darius ruled all Persia.
Yet *now* where are they? . . . Gone.

Gone where old Pythagorus gives
The square dance symmetry,
Where Sappho springs on heels of love
Besides a tideless sea.

Where Pharaohs do the sand-dance,
And Caesar reels through Gaul,
Salome dances on ahead,
While Hadrian foots his wall.

Where Chaucer treads his country dance
With Breugel at his heel,
Sir Walter Raleigh leads Queen Bess
In a Virginia Reel.

Nelson hops his hornpipe there,
Abel jigs with Seth.
Darwin does the fox-trot,
And Poe – his Dance of Death.

While Mozart plucks from paradise
Notes so sweet and just
That all our forebears dance . . . and we
Come dancing in their dust.

Terry Jones

BREAK DANCE

I'm going to break dance
turn rippling glass
stretch my muscles
to the bass

Whoo!

I'm going to break dance
I'm going to rip it
and jerk it
and take it apart

I'm going to chop it
and move it
and groove it

Ooooh I'm going to ooze it
electric boogaloo
electric boogaloo
across your floor

I'm going to break dance
watch my ass
take the shine
off your laugh

Whoo!

I'm going to dip it
and spin it
let my spine twist it
I'm going to shift it
and stride it
let my mind glide it

Then I'm going to ease it
ease it
and bring it all home
all home
            believing in the beat
            believing in the beat
            of myself

Grace Nichols

WHEN I DANCE

When I dance it isn't merely
That music absorbs my shyness,
My laughter settles in my eyes,
My swings of arms convert my frills
As timing tunes my feet with floor
As if I never just looked on.

It is that when I dance
O music expands my hearing
And it wants no mathematics,
It wants no thinking, no speaking,
It only wants all my feeling
In with animation of place.

When I dance it isn't merely
That surprises dictate movements,
Other rhythms move my rhythms,
I uncradle rocking-memory
And skipping, hopping and running
All mix movements I balance in.

It is that when I dance
I'm costumed in a rainbow mood,
I'm okay at any angle,
Outfit of drums crowds madness round,
Talking winds and plucked strings conspire,
Beat after beat warms me like sun.

When I dance it isn't merely
I shift bodyweight balances
As movement amasses my show,
I celebrate each dancer here,
No sleep invades me now at all
And I see how I am tireless.

It is that when I dance
I gather up all my senses
Well into hearing and feeling,
With body's flexible postures
Telling their poetry in movement
And I celebrate all rhythms.

James Berry

SCORE

Shadows of lampposts
stretch across the road.

If you could pluck one,
it would make a thick, deep sound.

Imagine you are travelling across the strings
of a huge grand piano.

Add to this the way leaf shadows
scrape the tarmac, softly,

and the high notes of the pavement
as it catches points of light.

Begin to hum a slow, free tune
you haven't heard before.

Wendy Cope

IF I WERE THE CONDUCTOR

If I were the conductor
Of an orchestra I'd choose
Piano-playing monkeys
And, as cellists, kangaroos,
A hippo on the piccolo,
A sloth on xylophone
And one giant, eight-legged octopus
Who'd play four flutes alone.

Richard Edwards

THE CEREMONIAL BAND

(To be said out loud by a chorus and solo voices)

The old King of Dorchester,
He had a little orchestra,
And never did you hear such a
                        ceremonial band.
  'Tootle-too,' said the flute,
  'Deed-a-reedle,' said the fiddle,
For the fiddles and the flutes were
                        the finest in the land.

The old King of Dorchester,
He had a little orchestra,
And never did you hear such a
                        ceremonial band.
  'Pump-a-rum,' said the drum,
  'Tootle-too,' said the flute,
  'Deed-a-reedle,' said the fiddle,
For the fiddles and the flutes were
                        the finest in the land.

The old King of Dorchester,
He had a little orchestra,
And never did you hear such a
                        ceremonial band.

'Pickle-pee,' said the fife,
'Pump-a-rum,' said the drum,
'Tootle-too,' said the flute,
'Deed-a-reedle,' said the fiddle,
For the fiddles and the flutes were
                    the finest in the land.

The old King of Dorchester,
He had a little orchestra,
And never did you hear such a
                    ceremonial band.
'Zoomba-zoom,' said the bass,
'Pickle-pee,' said the fife,
'Pump-a-rum,' said the drum,
'Tootle-too,' said the flute,
'Deed-a-reedle,' said the fiddle,
For the fiddles and the flutes were
                    the finest in the land.

The old King of Dorchester,
He had a little orchestra,
And never did you hear such a
                    ceremonial band.
'Pah-pa-rah,' said the trumpet,
'Zoomba-zoom,' said the bass,
'Pickle-pee,' said the fife,
'Pump-a-rum,' said the drum,
'Tootle-too,' said the flute,
'Deed-a-reedle,' said the fiddle,
For the fiddles and the flutes were
                    the finest in the land,
Oh! the fiddles and the flutes were
                    the finest in the land!

James Reeves

MUSIC MAKERS

My Auntie plays the piccolo,
My Uncle plays the flute,
They practise every night at ten
Tweetly tweet *Toot – toot*!

My Granny plays the banjo,
My Granddad plays the drum,
They practise every night at nine
Plankety plank *Bumm – bumm*!!

My sister plays the tuba,
My brother plays guitar,
They practise every night at six
Twankity *Oom – pa – pa*!!!

My mother plays the mouth organ,
My daddy plays oboe,
They practise every night at eight
Pompity-pom suck-blow!!!!

Spike Milligan

THE FIDDLER OF DOONEY

When I play on my fiddle in Dooney
Folk dance like a wave of the sea;
My cousin is priest in Kilvarnet,
My brother in Mocharabuiee.

I passed my brother and cousin:
They read in their books of prayer;
I read in my book of songs
I bought at the Sligo fair.

When we come at the end of time
To Peter sitting in state,
He will smile on the three old spirits,
But call me first through the gate;

For the good are always the merry,
Save by an evil chance,
And the merry love the fiddle,
And the merry love to dance:

And when the folk there spy me,
They will all come up to me,
With 'Here is the fiddler of Dooney!'
And dance like a wave of the sea.

W. B. Yeats

A MUSICAL INSTRUMENT

What was he doing, the great god Pan,
Down in the reeds by the river?
Spreading ruin and scattering ban,
Splashing and paddling with hoofs of a goat,
And breaking the golden lilies afloat
With the dragon-fly on the river.

He tore out a reed, the great god Pan,
From the deep cool bed of the river;
The limpid water turbidly ran,
And the broken lilies a-dying lay,
And the dragon-fly had fled away.
Ere he brought it out of the river.

High on the shore sat the great god Pan,
While turbidly flow'd the river;
And hack'd and hew'd as a great god can
With his hard bleak steel at the patient reed,
Till there was not a sign of the leaf indeed
To prove it fresh from the river.

He cut it short, did the great god Pan
(How tall it grew in the river!)
Then drew the pith, like the heart of a man,
Steadily, from the outside ring,
And notch'd the poor dry empty thing
In holes, as he sat by the river.

'This is the way,' laugh'd the great god Pan
(Laugh'd while he sat by the river),
'The only way, since gods began
To make sweet music, they could succeed.'
Then dropping his mouth to a hole in the reed,
He blew in power by the river.

Sweet, sweet, sweet, O Pan!
Piercing sweet by the river!
Blinding sweet, O great god Pan!
The sun on the hill forgot to die,
And the lilies revived, and the dragon-fly
Came back to dream on the river.

Yet half a beast is the great god Pan,
To laugh as he sits by the river,
Making a poet out of a man:
The true gods sigh for the cost and pain –
For the reed which grows nevermore again
As a reed with the reeds of the river.

Elizabeth Barrett Browning

FANTASY

What's your favourite fantasy? We all have them. Even as I walk down the street, I fantasise about doing the most extraordinary things – something incredibly brave, for instance, like stopping an armed robbery single-handed. (It's amazing how I manage to disarm three or four desperate men without getting my glasses broken, but there you are.) Gateways tempt me to imagine that perfect goal that wins us the World Cup, and I'm forever slogging fast bowlers back over their head for six as I walk along the pavement.

One day I'll probably get run over or walk into a lamp-post. But until that happens I'll continue to enjoy my fantasies. We all need that element of 'if only' in our lives, as Richard Edwards knows. Personally I wouldn't particularly want to be an astronomer or an explorer, and his train driver gets a long way off the beaten track. But there are a number of other things I would like to be. How about you?

I'm sure fantasies are very healthy from a psychological point of view. Each of us needs to feel like the most important person in the world from time to time to make up for all the occasions when people put us down. But fantasies are also very valuable from a creative point of view. Imagination needs to be used to develop and fantasies, by definition, exercise the imagination pretty rigorously. No one shows this more clearly than Samuel Taylor Coleridge in his poem 'Kubla Khan', with its rhythmical excitement and breathtaking magical scenery:

> Five miles meandering with a mazy motion
> Through wood and dale the sacred river ran,
> Then reached the caverns measureless to man,
> And sank in tumult to a lifeless ocean . . .

The story behind the poem is that Coleridge dreamed it – not just the vision, but the actual words used in the poem – and he was busy writing it down as though from dictation when he was interrupted by a person from Porlock arriving at the door to talk about something humdrum like the plumbing. The rest of the poem then slipped from Coleridge's mind. Perhaps really he just got stuck and the interruption was a useful fantasy! Whatever really happened, the thought of more marvellous poetry being lost always adds a touch of poignancy to 'Kubla Khan' for me.

Fantasy offers a huge scope to the writer. Anything and everything is allowed. Irene Rawnsley's poem 'Fisherman's Tale' treats extraordinary events as though they were normal, and we stay with aquatic life with what must be one of the most extraordinary dances ever dreamed of, Lewis Carroll's 'The Lobster Quadrille', from one of the greatest fantasy books of all time, *Alice in Wonderland*:

'Will you walk a little faster?' said a whiting to a snail.
'There's a porpoise close behind us, and he's treading on my tail.
See how eagerly the lobsters and the turtles all advance!
They are waiting on the shingle – will you come and join the dance?'

Now, though most fantasies are private and deeply personal to the person having them, every now and then you can share a fantasy. That's what I like about Gareth Owen's 'Shed in Space' – the way the grandson and grandfather join in the same fantasy (though it still remains private to them):

And so we'd fly,
Through timeless afternoons
Till tea time came,
Among the planets
And mysterious suns,
While the world
receded like a dream . . .

IF I WERE AN ASTRONOMER

If I were an astronomer
I'd scan the skies all night,
Till, through my great big telescope,
A planet spun in sight,
A planet full of bug-eyed men,
As green as green could be,
Who, through their great big telescopes,
Stared goggling back at me.

Richard Edwards

IF I WERE AN EXPLORER

If I were an explorer
I'd reach that far-off land
Called Jumbledup, where sand was sea
And sea was made of sand,
Where snow fell every summer
On herds of grazing bees,
And cows flew round the blossom
Of the orange apple trees.

Richard Edwards

IF ONLY I COULD DRIVE A TRAIN

If only I could drive a train
I'd fit it with computers
And take off on a mystery tour
To startle bored commuters,
And how they'd gaze and mutter
As we flew between the stars
To pull in, only two hours late,
At platform four on Mars.

Richard Edwards

TONIGHT AT NOON*

(for Charlie Mingus and the Clayton Squares)

Tonight at noon
Supermarkets will advertise 3d EXTRA on everything
Tonight at noon
Children from happy families will be sent to live in a
    home
Elephants will tell each other human jokes
America will declare peace on Russia
World War I generals will sell poppies in the streets on
    November 11th
The first daffodils of autumn will appear
When the leaves fall upwards to the trees

Tonight at noon
Pigeons will hunt cats through city backyards
Hitler will tell us to fight on the beaches and on the
    landing fields
A tunnel full of water will be built under Liverpool
Pigs will be sighted flying in formation over Woolton
and Nelson will not only get his eye back but his arm as
    well
White Americans will demonstrate for equal rights
in front of the Black House
and the Monster has just created Dr Frankenstein

Girls in bikinis are moonbathing
Folksongs are being sung by real folk
Art galleries are closed to people over 21
Poets get their poems in the Top 20
Politicians are elected to insane asylums
There's jobs for everyone and nobody wants them
In back alleys everywhere teenage lovers are kissing
in broad daylight.

In forgotten graveyards the dead will quietly bury the
    living
and
You will tell me you love me
Tonight at noon.

Adrian Henri

* *The title for this poem is taken from an LP by Charlie Mingus, 'Tonight At Noon'*

FISHERMAN'S TALE

By the canal
I was quietly fishing
when a bowler hat
floated by,
stopped level with my eye
and began to rise.

Below it was a man's head
wearing spectacles;
he asked,
'This way to Brackley?'
'Straight ahead.'
The face sank back
beneath the wet,
but I was thinking
Brackley's seven miles,
it's getting late;
perhaps he doesn't know
how far.

I tapped the hat
with my rod; again
the face rose; 'Yes?'
'You'll need to hurry
to arrive before dark.'
'Don't worry,' he said;
I'm on my bike.'

Irene Rawnsley

ANY PRINCE TO ANY PRINCESS

August is coming
and the goose, I'm afraid,
is getting fat.
There have been
no golden eggs for some months now.
Straw has fallen well below market price
despite my frantic spinning
and the sedge is,
as you rightly point out,
withered.

I can't imagine how the pea
got under your mattress. I apologize
humbly. The chambermaid has, of course,
been sacked. As has the frog footman.
I understand that, during my recent fact-finding tour of
    the Golden River,
despite your nightly unavailing efforts,
he remained obstinately
froggish.

I hope that the Three Wishes granted by the General
    Assembly
will go some way towards redressing
this unfortunate recent sequence of events.
The fall in output from the shoe-factory, for example:
no one could have foreseen the work-to-rule
by the National Union of Elves. Not to mention the fact
that the court has been fast asleep
for the last six and a half years.
The matter of the poisoned apple has been taken up
by the Board of Trade: I think I can assure you
the incident will not be
repeated.

I can quite understand, in the circumstances,
your reluctance to let down
your golden tresses. However
I feel I must point out
that the weather isn't getting any better

and I already have a nasty chill
from waiting at the base
of the White Tower. You must see
the absurdity of the situation.
Some of the courtiers are beginning to talk,
not to mention the humble villagers.
It's been three weeks now, and not even
a word.

Princess,
a cold, black wind
howls through our empty palace.
Dead leaves litter the bedchamber;
the mirror on the wall hasn't said a thing
since you left. I can only ask,
bearing all this in mind,
that you think again,

let down your hair,

reconsider.

Adrian Henri

THE LOBSTER QUADRILLE

'Will you walk a little faster?' said a whiting to a snail.
'There's a porpoise close behind us, and he's treading on
    my tail.
See how eagerly the lobsters and the turtles all advance!
They are waiting on the shingle – will you come and join
    the dance?
  Will you, won't you, will you, won't you, will you join
    the dance?
  Will you, won't you, will you, won't you, won't you
    join the dance?

'You can really have no notion how delightful it will be
When they take us up and throw us, with the lobsters,
    out to sea!'
But the snail replied 'Too far, too far!' and gave a look
    askance –

Said he thanked the whiting kindly, but he would
    not join the dance.
  Would not, could not, would not, could not, would
    not join the dance.
  Would not, could not, would not, could not, could not
    join the dance.

'What matters it how far we go?' his scaly friend replied.
'There is another shore, you know, upon the other side.
The further off from England the nearer is to France –
Then turn not pale, beloved snail, but come and join the
    dance.
  Will you, won't you, will you, won't you, will you join
    the dance?
  Will you, won't you, will you, won't you, won't you
    join the dance?'

Lewis Carroll

THROUGH THAT DOOR

Through that door
Is a garden with a wall,
The red brick crumbling,
The lupins growing tall,
Where the lawn is like a carpet
Spread for you,
And it's all as tranquil
As you never knew.

Through that door
Is the great ocean-sea
Which heaves and rolls
To eternity,
With its islands and promontories
Waiting for you
To explore and discover
In that vastness of blue.

Through that door
Is your secret room
Where the window lets in
The light of the moon,
With its mysteries and magic
Where you can find
Thrills and excitements
of every kind.

Through that door
Are the mountains and the moors
And the rivers and the forests
Of the great outdoors,
All the plains and the ice-caps
And the lakes as blue as sky
For all those creatures
That walk or swim or fly.

Through that door
Is the city of the mind
Where you can imagine
What you'll find.
You can make of that city
What you want it to,
And if you choose to share it,
Then it could come true.

John Cotton

KUBLA KHAN

In Xanadu did Kubla Khan
A stately pleasure-dome decree:
Where Alph, the sacred river, ran
Through caverns measureless to man
    Down to a sunless sea.
So twice five miles of fertile ground
With walls and towers were girdled round:
And there were gardens bright with sinuous rills,
Where blossomed many an incense-bearing tree;
And here were forests ancient as the hills,
Enfolding sunny spots of greenery.

But oh! that deep romantic chasm which slanted
Down the green hill athwart a cedarn cover!
A savage place! as holy and enchanted
As e'er beneath a waning moon was haunted
By woman wailing for her demon-lover!
And from this chasm, with ceaseless turmoil seething,
As if this earth in fast thick pants were breathing,
A mighty fountain momently was forced:
Amid whose swift half-intermitted burst
Huge fragments vaulted like rebounding hail,
Or chaffy grain beneath the thresher's flail:
And 'mid these dancing rocks at once and ever
It flung up momently the sacred river.
Five miles meandering with a mazy motion
Through wood and dale the sacred river ran,
Then reached the caverns measureless to man,
And sank in tumult to a lifeless ocean:
And 'mid this tumult Kubla heard from far
Ancestral voices prophesying war!
    The shadow of the dome of pleasure
    Floated midway on the waves;
    Where was heard the mingled measure
    From the fountain and the caves.
It was a miracle of rare device,
A sunny pleasure-dome with caves of ice!

A damsel with a dulcimer
In a vision once I saw:
It was an Abyssinian maid,
And on her dulcimer she played,
Singing of Mount Abora.
Could I revive within me
Her symphony and song,
To such a deep delight 'twould win me,
That with music loud and long,
I would build that dome in air,
That sunny dome! those caves of ice!
And all who heard should see them there,
And all should cry, Beware! Beware!
His flashing eyes, his floating hair!
Weave a circle round him thrice,
And close your eyes with holy dread,
For he on honey-dew hath fed,
And drunk the milk of Paradise.

Samuel Taylor Coleridge

BILLY DREAMER'S FANTASTIC FRIENDS

The Incredible Hulk came to tea.
Robin was with him too,
Batman stayed at home that night
Because his bat had flu.

Superman called to say hello
And Spiderman spun us a joke.
Dynamite Sue was supposed to come
But she went up in smoke.

The Invisible Man might have called,
But as I wasn't sure,
I left an empty chair and bun
Beside the kitchen door.

They signed my autograph book.
But I dropped it in the fire.
Now whenever I tell my friends
They say I'm a terrible liar.

But incredible people *do* call round
('Specially when I'm alone),
And if they don't, and I get bored,
I call them on the phone.

Brian Patten

SHED IN SPACE

My Grandad Lewis
On my mother's side
Had two ambitions.
One was to take first prize
For shallots at the village show
And the second
Was to be a space commander.

Every Tuesday
After I'd got their messages,
He'd lead me with a wink
To his garden shed
And there, amongst the linseed
And the sacks of peat and horse manure
He'd light his pipe
And settle in his deck chair.
His old eyes on the blue and distant
That no one else could see,
He'd ask,
'Are we A O.K. for lift off?'
Gripping the handles of the lawn mower
I'd reply:
'A O.K.'

And then
Facing the workbench,
In front of shelves of paint and creosote
And racks of glistening chisels
He'd talk to Mission Control.
'Five-Four-Three-Two-One-Zero –
We have lift off.
This is Grandad Lewis talking,
Do you read me?
Britain's first space shed
is rising majestically into orbit
From its launch pad
In the allotments
In Lakey Lane.'

And so we'd fly,
Through timeless afternoons
Till tea time came,
Amongst the planets
And mysterious suns,
While the world
Receded like a dream:
Grandad never won
That prize for shallots,
But as the captain
Of an intergalactic shed
There was no one to touch him.

Gareth Owen

WHAT IS IT?

there's a creak from the cupboard
there's a scratch on the door
sometimes the roof groans
sometimes the floor

Mother says it's just because
the house is very old
Dad says it's the wind
and I'm always being told
that I should be more sensible
use less imagination
but that's the way
I find out things
a sort of education

and only I know
what it is
that's making the house shake
only I can recognise
the noise
a finger makes
when it's scritching
on a window
or scrabbling to get in

only I know what it is
that's creeping round
outside
that's waiting
for an opening
to slither
and to glide
into the house

Joan Poulson

CATS

From my study window I can see the cats in my road slinking under cars and hedges, parading along walls and swaggering down garden paths. Every cat has a distinctive character of its own and watching the ups and downs of street cat life is better than a TV soap. Their behaviour seems so human, it's easy to think of them as little people in fur coats passing comments to each other about us. In 'Conversation on a Garden Wall', Adrian Henri imagines a couple of cats chatting on a garden wall about the peculiar habits of their owners:

. . . All mine do is sit in front of a little box with tiny ones inside it.

Of course, that's just what a telly must look like to a cat! My cat ignores the television but is fascinated by baths. She sits by the taps looking at me as if I was completely mad. Or that's what it seems like, but of course cats don't think like people, they think like . . . well . . . cats! You just try thinking like a cat. It's very hard, you have to forget almost everything you know about the world, because a cat only knows the little patch of house and garden that it sees every day. They notice things that we wouldn't because their senses are sharper than ours, but they can't work things out as we can because they aren't as clever. To a cat even snowflakes are incomprehensible, they look a bit like insects but feel funny on the paws:

They have no body and no buzz.
And now his feet are wet:
it's a puzzle.

'Cat and the Weather' by May Swenson

I wonder what my city-born cat thought when she met a cow for the first time when we moved to the country. She certainly knew what to think when she ran into a fox – straight through the cat flap at a hundred miles an hour and under the bed! Her instinct told her what to do because every cat, including the fattest, fluffiest Persian pedigree, leads a double life. Half of the time they're a domestic pet and half of the time a wild animal. I'm sure that ability to become wild the moment they step outside the back door was what earned them a reputation as witches' familiars, friends of the magical moon just like Minnaloushe, the cat in W. B. Yeats' poem, 'The Cat and the Moon':

> Minnaloushe creeps through the grass
> Alone, important and wise,
> And lifts to the changing moon
> His changing eyes.

It's the untamed part of cats that I love, and spying on my old moggy as she stalks and pounces in the long grass gives me the greatest pleasure. She is transformed – no longer furry, floppy, foot-warmer but tortoiseshell tiger, striking terror into the hearts of shrews, a miniature big cat like the ones in the jungles of India:

> Tiger, tiger, burning bright
> In the forests of the night,

'The Tiger' by William Blake

FIVE EYES

In Hans' old mill his three black cats
Watch his bins for the thieving rats.
Whisker and claw, they crouch in the night,
Their five eyes smouldering green and bright:
Squeaks from the flour sacks, squeaks from where
The cold wind stirs on the empty stair,
Squeaking and scampering, everywhere.
Then down they pounce, now in, now out,
At whisking tail, and sniffing snout;
While lean old Hans he snores away
Till peep of light at break of day;
Then up he climbs to his creaking mill,
Out come his cats all grey with meal –
Jekkel, and Jessup, and one-eyed Jill.

Walter de la Mare

TWO LITTLE KITTENS

Two little kittens, one stormy night,
Began to quarrel, and then to fight;
One had a mouse, the other had none,
And that's the way the quarrel begun.

'I'll have that mouse,' said the biggest cat;
'You'll have that mouse? We'll see about that!'
'I *will* have that mouse,' said the eldest son;
'You *shan't* have the mouse,' said the little one.

I told you before 'twas a stormy night
When these two little kittens began to fight;
The old woman seized her sweeping broom,
And swept the two kittens right out of the room.

The ground was covered with frost and snow,
And the two little kittens had nowhere to go;
So they laid them down on the mat at the door,
While the old woman finished sweeping the floor.

Then they crept in, as quiet as mice,
All wet with the snow, and as cold as ice,
For they found it was better, that stormy night,
To lie down and sleep than to quarrel and fight.

Anon.

CONVERSATION ON A GARDEN WALL

Move over, you've got all the bricks with the sun on.
Oh, all right. Mind you. I was here first.
He came round after me again last night. Right up to the
back door.
Really? He's persistent, I'll say that for him.
I'll say. Anyway, they chased him away.
How are yours treating you?
Not too bad, really. They're a bit careful with the milk.
Oh, mine are all right about that. They're a bit
unimaginative with my food, though. Last week I had the
same meal every day.
You don't say. The food's O.K. It's a real pain being pushed
out in the rain. Every night, rain or snow, out I go.
Me too. Look, here he is back again.
Cheek. Pretend to take no notice.
At least you've got a quiet place with none of those small
ones around. I hardly get a minute.
That's true. All mine do is sit in front of a little box with tiny
ones inside it.
Mine do too. It's the only peace I get.
And one of them pushes that noisy thing round the floor
every day.
Terrible, isn't it? Mind you, mine only does it once or twice
a week.
You're lucky. Oh, the sun's gone in.
Yes, time for a stroll. I'll jump down and just sort of walk
past him, accidentally.
Accidentally on purpose, you mean. See you around.
Yes, see you around. I'll tell you one thing, though.
What's that?
It's a good job they can't talk, isn't it?

Adrian Henri

PUSSY CAT, PUSSY CAT

Pussy cat, pussy cat,
Where have you been?
I went to London
To see the queen.
Pussy cat, pussy cat,
What did you see?
I saw a policeman
Following me.
Pussy cat, pussy cat,
What did he do?
He said to me,
'Home you go!
Shoo, shoo, shoo!'

Spike Milligan

MACAVITY: THE MYSTERY CAT

Macavity's a Mystery Cat: he's called the Hidden Paw –
For he's the master criminal who can defy the Law.
He's the bafflement of Scotland Yard, the Flying Squad's
     despair:
For when they reach the scene of crime – *Macavity's not
     there*!

Macavity, Macavity, there's no one like Macavity,
He's broken every human law, he breaks the law of gravity.
His powers of levitation would make a fakir stare,
And when you reach the scene of crime – *Macavity's not
     there*!
You may seek him in the basement, you may look up in the
     air –
But I tell you once and once again, *Macavity's not there*!

Macavity's a ginger cat, he's very tall and thin;
You would know him if you saw him, for his eyes are
     sunken in.
His brow is deeply lined with thought, his head is highly
     domed;

His coat is dusty from neglect, his whiskers are uncombed.
He sways his head from side to side, with movements like a
    snake;
And when you think he's half asleep, he's always wide
    awake.

Macavity, Macavity, there's no one like Macavity,
For he's a fiend in feline shape, a monster of depravity.
You may meet him in a by-street, you may see him in the
    square –
But when a crime's discovered, then *Macavity's not there*!

He's outwardly respectable. (They say he cheats at cards.)
And his footprints are not found in any file of Scotland
    Yard's.
And when the larder's looted, or the jewel-case is rifled,
Or when the milk is missing, or another Peke's been stifled,
Or the greenhouse glass is broken, and the trellis past repair –
Ay, there's the wonder of the thing! *Macavity's not there*!

And when the Foreign Office find a Treaty's gone astray,
Or the Admiralty lose some plans and drawings by the way,
There may be a scrap of paper in the hall or on the stair –
But it's useless to investigate – *Macavity's not there*!
And when the loss has been disclosed, the Secret Service say:
'It *must* have been Macavity!' – but he's a mile away.
You'll be sure to find him resting, or a-licking of his thumbs,
Or engaged in doing complicated long division sums.

Macavity, Macavity, there's no one like Macavity,
There never was a Cat of such deceitfulness and suavity.
He always has an alibi, and one or two to spare:
At whatever time the deed took place – MACAVITY WASN'T
    THERE!
And they say that all the Cats whose wicked deeds are
    widely known
(I might mention Mungojerrie, I might mention
    Griddlebone)
Are nothing more than agents for the Cat who all the time
Just controls their operations: the Napoleon of Crime!

T. S. Eliot

THE GALLOPING CAT

Oh I am a cat that likes to
Gallop about doing good
So
One day when I was
Galloping about doing good, I saw
A Figure in the path; I said:
Get off! (Be-
cause
I am a cat that likes to
Gallop about doing good)
But he did not move, instead
He raised his hand as if
To land me a cuff
So I made to dodge so as to
Prevent him bringing it orf,
Un-for-tune-ately I slid
On a banana skin
Some Ass had left instead
Of putting in the bin. So
His hand caught me on the cheek
I tried
To lay his arm open from wrist to elbow
With my sharp teeth
Because I am
A cat that likes to gallop about doing good.
Would you believe it?
He wasn't there
My teeth met nothing but air,
But a Voice said: Poor cat,
(Meaning me) and a soft stroke
Came on me head
Since when
I have been bald.
I regard myself as
A martyr to doing good.
Also I heard a swoosh
As of wings, and saw
A halo shining at the height of
Mrs Gubbins's backyard fence,

So I thought: What's the good
Of galloping about doing good
When angels stand in the path
And do not do as they should
Such as having an arm to be bitten off
All the same I
Intend to go on being
A cat that likes to
Gallop about doing good
So
Now with my bald head I go,
Chopping the untidy flowers down, to
    and fro,
An' scooping up the grass to show
Underneath
The cinder path of wrath
Ha ha ha ha, ho,
Angels aren't the only ones who do
    not know
What's what and that
Galloping about doing good
Is a full-time job
That needs
An experienced eye of earthly
Sharpness, worth I dare say
(If you'll forgive a personal note)
A good deal more
Than all that skyey stuff
Of angels that make so bold as
To pity a cat like me that
Gallops about doing good.

Stevie Smith

COURAGE

Courage is when you're
allergic to cats and

your new friend says can
you come to her house to
play after school and

stay to dinner then
maybe go skating and
sleep overnight? And,

she adds, you can pet
her small kittens! Oh,
how you ache to. It

takes courage to
say 'no' to all that.

Emily Hearn

CAT AND THE WEATHER

Cat takes a look at the weather.
Snow.
Puts a paw on the sill.
His perch is piled, is a pillow.

Shape of his pad appears.
Will it dig? No.
Not like sand.
Like his fur almost.

But licked, not liked,
Too cold.
Insects are flying, fainting down.
He'll try

to bat one against the pane.
They have no body and no buzz.
And now his feet are wet:
it's a puzzle.

Shakes each leg,
then shakes his skin
to get the white flies off.
looks for his tail,

tells it to come on in
by the radiator.
World's turned queer
somehow. All white,

no smell. Well, here
inside it's still familiar.
He'll go to sleep until
it puts itself right.

May Swenson

THE CAT AND THE MOON

The cat went here and there
And the moon spun round like a top,
And the nearest kin of the moon,
The creeping cat, looked up.
Black Minnaloushe stared at the moon,
For, wander and wail as he would,
The pure cold light in the sky
Troubled his animal blood.
Minnaloushe runs in the grass
Lifting his delicate feet.
Do you dance, Minnaloushe, do you dance?
When two close kindred meet,
What better than call a dance?
Maybe the moon may learn,
Tired of that courtly fashion,
A new dance turn.

Minnaloushe creeps through the grass
From moonlit place to place,
The sacred moon overhead
Has taken a new phase.
Does Minnaloushe know that his pupils
Will pass from change to change,
And that from round to crescent,
From crescent to round they range?
Minnaloushe creeps through the grass
Alone, important and wise,
And lifts to the changing moon
His changing eyes.

W.B. Yeats

TIGER

Tiger, tiger, in the night
How can you see without a light?
To separate your foes from friendes
Are you wearing contact lenses?
Remember, tho', he's from the jungle –
He once ate my Aunt and Ungle
Eating people isn't nice:
Wouldn't you rather curry and rice?
So in your suit of striped pyjamas
Promise you will never harm us.
If you say you don't give a hoot, you
See, someone will have to shoot you!

Spike Milligan

THE TIGER

Tiger, tiger, burning bright
In the forests of the night,
What immortal hand or eye
Could frame thy fearful symmetry?

In what distant deeps or skies
Burnt the fire of thine eyes?
On what wings dare he aspire?
What the hand dare seize the fire?

And what shoulder and what art
Could twist the sinews of thy heart?
And, when thy heart began to beat,
What dread hand and what dread feet?

What the hammer? What the chain?
In what furnace was thy brain?
What the anvil? What dread grasp
Dare its deadly terrors clasp?

When the stars threw down their spears,
And water'd heaven with their tears,
Did He smile his work to see?
Did He who made the lamb make thee?

Tiger, tiger, burning bright
In the forests of the night,
What immortal hand or eye
Dare frame thy fearful symmetry?

William Blake

SECOND GLANCE AT A JAGUAR

Skinful of bowls, he bowls them,
The hip going in and out of joint, dropping the spine
With the urgency of his hurry
Like a cat going along under thrown stones, under cover,
Glancing sideways, running
Under his spine. A terrible, stump-legged waddle
Like a thick Aztec disemboweller,
Club-swinging, trying to grind some square
Socket between his hind legs round,
Carrying his head like a brazier of spilling embers,
And the black bit of his mouth, he takes it
Between his back teeth, he has to wear his skin out,
He swipes a lap at the water-trough as he turns,
Swivelling the ball of his heel on the polished spot,
Showing his belly like a butterfly
At every stride he has to turn a corner
In himself and correct it. His head
Is like the worn down stump of another whole jaguar,
His body is just the engine shoving it forward,
Lifting the air up and shoving on under,
The weight of his fangs hanging the mouth open,
Bottom jaw combing the ground. A gorged look,
Gangster, club-tail lumped along behind gracelessly,
He's wearing himself to heavy ovals,
Muttering some mantrah, some drum-song of murder
To keep his rage brightening, making his skin
Intolerable, spurred by the rosettes, the cain-brands,
Wearing the spots off from the inside,
Rounding some revenge. Going like a prayer-wheel,
The head dragging forward, the body keeping up,
The hind legs lagging. He coils, he flourishes
The blackjack tail as if looking for a target,
Hurrying through the underworld, soundless.

Ted Hughes

THE ENVIRONMENT

That rather pompous-sounding word 'environment' simply means 'surroundings' but it is used to convey so much more. Environment has become a green word. We talk about 'environment-friendly products', 'dangers to the environment' and 'environment ministers' meet to discuss the future of our planet. When I hear that word I think of pollution and burning forests. We humans have done terrible things to our 'surroundings', our 'environment', our lovely home, Earth. Even in Thomas Hardy's time, more than a hundred years ago, it was happening. Hardy was shocked at how quickly humans could destroy what had taken so long to create:

The tree crashes downward: it shakes all its neighbours throughout,
And two hundred years' steady growth has been ended in less than two hours.

Of course, now we are sending whole species crashing down into extinction, sending hundreds of millions of years of evolution into oblivion. The pace of destruction is frightening and it has inspired some pretty gloomy views of the future – a world where walking on grass is only a memory in Gordon Macintosh's 'To Walk on Grass', or where Britain's last rabbit is kept behind barbed wire, in Alan Brownjohn's 'We Are Going to See the Rabbit'. But those are only cautionary tales. We could stop the destruction now and our planet could heal. Earth has great powers of recovery, a feeling that Vachel Lindsay catches in the last lines of 'The Flower-Fed Buffaloes' where he describes the almost extinct herds of buffalo and tribes of Indians as 'lying low', implying a day of return and recuperation.

I find I need to fight off the sense of hopelessness that the word 'environment' is beginning to trigger in me. I need poems that celebrate the other meanings of environment – the green, the growing, wings and paws and fur and feather. Tennyson's 'The Eagle' is a great hope-restorer and I challenge anyone to read it without feeling their heart turn over or hearing the rush of wind on the last lines:

> He watches from his mountain walls,
> And like a thunderbolt he falls.

Perhaps what we all need are some positive visions of what the world could be like if we grew forests instead of hamburgers and used our legs instead of burning petrol in cars. Perhaps we should all write about a future full of animals and greenery and take the last line of Hopkins' 'Inversnaid' as our rallying cry:

> Long live the weeds and the wilderness yet.

EXTINCTION OF THE 21ST CENTURY DODO

(For the Dodo think Whale, Fox, Badger etc)

The Dodo said
to the kangaroo
I wish I could jump
and skip away like you

The Dodo said
to the goat and the ape
I wish I could climb
so I can escape

The Dodo said
to the birds in the trees
I wish I could fly
and float in the breeze

The Dodo said
to the fish in the sea
I wish I could swim
so I could be free

The Dodo said
to the ant and the mole
I wish I was small
so I could hide in a hole

The Dodo said
to the man with a gun
why do you kill me
just for fun?

The Dodo said
to God in Heaven
why'd you let man
invent that weapon?

J. Walsh

TO WALK ON GRASS

I remember what it was
to walk on grass
I remember when they used to
count the years
and number them
one by one. One after the next
An interesting tale
but no one to tell it to

And words like *crowds*,
and *birds* and *life* I recall
they never used to frighten me.

If only there was someone
who could remind me
what colours were
If only I could tell them in return
what it was
to walk on grass.

Gordon Macintosh

THE FLOWER-FED BUFFALOES

The flower-fed buffaloes of the spring
In the days of long ago,
Ranged where the locomotives sing
And the prairie flowers lie low:–
The tossing, blooming, perfumed grass
Is swept away by the wheat,
Wheels and wheels and wheels spin by
In the spring that still is sweet.
But the flower-fed buffaloes of the spring
Left us, long ago.
They gore no more, they bellow no more,
They trundle around the hills no more:–
With the Blackfeet, lying low,
With the Pawnees, lying low,
Lying low.

Vachel Lindsay

HARVEST HYMN

We spray the fields and scatter
   The poison on the ground
So that no wicked wild flowers
   Upon our farm be found.
We like whatever helps us
   To line our purse with pence;
The twenty-four-hour broiler-house
   And neat electric fence.

   All concrete sheds around us
      And Jaguars in the yard,
   The telly lounge and deep-freeze
      Are ours from working hard.

We fire the fields for harvest,
   The hedges swell the flame,
The oak trees and the cottages
   From which our fathers came.
We give no compensation,
   The earth is ours today,
And if we lose on arable,
   Then bungalows will pay.

   All concrete sheds . . . etc.

John Betjeman

STANTON DREW

First you dismantle the landscape.
Take away everything you first
Thought of. Trees must go,
Roads, of course, the church,
Houses, hedges, livestock, a wire
Fence. The river can stay,
But loses its stubby fringe
Of willows. What do you
See now? Grass, the circling
Mendip rim, with its notches
Fresh, like carving. A sky
Like ours, but empty along
Its lower levels. And earth
Stripped of its future, tilted
Into meaning by these stones,
Pitted and unemphatic. Re-create them.
They are the most permanent
Presences here, but cattle, weather,
Archaeologists have rubbed against
    them.
Still in season they will
Hold the winter sun poised
Over Maes Knoll's white cheek,
Chain the moon's footsteps to
The pattern of their dance.
Stand inside the circle. Put
Your hand on stone. Listen
To the past's long pulse.

                    U. A. Fanthorpe

THROWING A TREE

New Forest

The two executioners stalk along over the knolls,
Bearing two axes with heavy heads shining and wide,
And a long limp two-handled saw toothed for cutting
   great boles,
And so they approach the proud tree that bears the death-
   mark on its side.

Jackets doffed they swing axes and chop away just
   above ground,
And the chips fly about and lie white on the moss and
   fallen leaves;
Till a broad deep gash in the bark is hewn all the way
   round,
And one of them tries to hook upward a rope, which at
   last he achieves.

The saw then begins, till the top of the tall giant
   shivers:
The shivers are seen to grow greater each cut than
   before:
They edge out the saw, tug the rope; but the tree only
   quivers,
And kneeling and sawing again, they step back to try
   pulling once more.

Then, lastly, the living mast sways, further sways: with
   a shout
Job and Ike rush aside. Reached the end of its long
   staying powers
The tree crashes downward: it shakes all its
   neighbours throughout,
And two hundred years' steady growth has been ended in
   less than two hours.

Thomas Hardy

THE EAGLE

He clasps the crag with crooked hands:
Close to the sun in lonely lands,
Ringed with the azure world, he stands.

The wrinkled sea beneath him crawls;
He watches from his mountain walls,
And like a thunderbolt he falls.

Alfred Lord Tennyson

I GET HIGH ON BUTTERFLIES

I get high on butterflies;
the way they loom in the air
and land on air-dromes
                    of petals

and with nervous wings
shake off their colours
                    of orange, green and blue. . .

I get high on butterflies;
their very names:
                    Tiger swallow tail
                    Zebra
                    Pygmy blue
                    Arctic skipper
                    Spring azure
                    Common wood nymph.

Caught in the net of my mind
they whirl around
                    and around. . .

Joe Rosenblatt

THE HAWK

Afternoon,
with just enough of a breeze
        for him to ride it
lazily, a hawk
sails still-winged
up the slope of a stubble-covered hill,
so low
he nearly
touches his shadow

Robert Sund

'WE ARE GOING TO
SEE THE RABBIT . . .'

We are going to see the rabbit,
We are going to see the rabbit.
Which rabbit, people say?
Which rabbit, ask the children?
Which rabbit,
The only rabbit,
The only rabbit in England,
Sitting behind a barbed-wire fence
Under the floodlights, neon lights,
Sodium lights,
Nibbling grass
On the only patch of grass
In England, in England
(Except the grass by the hoardings
Which doesn't count.)
We are going to see the rabbit
And we must be there on time.

First we shall go by escalator,
Then we shall go by underground,
And then we shall go by motorway
And then by helicopterway,
And the last ten yards we shall have to go
On foot.

And now we are going
All the way to see the rabbit,
We are nearly there,
We are longing to see it,
And so is the crowd
Which is here in thousands
With mounted policemen
And big loudspeakers
And bands and banners,
And everyone has come a long way.
But soon we shall see it
Sitting and nibbling
The blades of grass
On the only patch of grass
In – but something has gone wrong!
Why is everyone so angry,
Why is everyone jostling
And slanging and complaining?
The rabbit has gone,
Yes, the rabbit has gone
He has actually burrowed down into the earth
And made himself a warren, under the earth,
Despite all these people.
And what shall we do?
What *can* we do?

It is all a pity, you must be disappointed,
Go home and do something else for today,
Go home again, go home for today.
For you cannot hear the rabbit, under the earth,
Remarking rather sadly to himself, by himself,
As he rests in his warren, under the earth:
'It won't be long, they are bound to come,
They are bound to come and find me, even here.'

Alan Brownjohn

INVERSNAID

This darksome burn, horseback brown,
His rollrock highroad roaring down,
In coop and in comb the fleece of his foam
Flutes and low to the lake falls home.

A windpuff-bonnet of fawn-froth
Turns and twindles over the broth
Of a pool so pitchblack, fell-frowning,
It rounds and rounds Despair to drowning.

Degged with dew, dappled with dew
Are the groins of the braes that the brook treads
    through,
Wiry heathpacks, flitches of fern,
And the beadbonny ash that sits over the burn.

What would the world be, once bereft
Of wet and of wildness? Let them be left,
O let them be left, wildness and wet;
Long live the weeds and the wilderness yet.

Gerard Manley Hopkins

THE WHALER

A whaler was a-whaling
In the deep North Sea,
Wiping out endangered species
As busy as could be.

They didn't give a tootle
What sort of whales they shot:
Bowheads, Humpbacks, Sperm and Blue Whales –
They simply bagged the lot!

Mother whales and babies
– They'd no time for regrets –
They slaughtered whole herds at a time
To sell as food for pets.

When suddenly they saw a whale
Bigger than the rest,
And the Captain yelled: 'Let's get her, boys!
She's got to be the best!'

So they started chasing after
That extraordinary whale,
And they didn't stop their engines
Till they'd caught up with its tail,

Then they fired off their harpoon,
With its explosive head,
And the thing exploded in the beast
And should have killed it dead.

But the creature thrashed and turned on them,
And gave a sort of 'cluck!',
And the Captain screamed: 'That's not a whale!
My boys! It's Moby Duck!'

But Moby Duck closed in on them
– Rage written on his face –
His huge beak snapping at their stern,
As they began to race.

He chased them through the North Sea,
There was nothing they could do,
For he caught them and in moments
He had pecked their boat in two.

They scrambled for the lifeboats,
And they lived to tell the tale,
But those whalers never ever
Tried to kill another whale.

And what of Moby Duck, my friends?
Ah! but who can say?
He swam into the sunset
To quack another day.

Terry Jones

CONFLICT

We all know about conflict on one scale or another. Do you have rows with your brother or sister? School friends? Parents? Most people do. How do conflicts start? Often, obviously, with an act of aggression. I want that, and I'm going to take it. What are you going to do about it? But conflicts also arise through misunderstandings – sometimes deliberate. The saying is that it takes two to start a quarrel, and quite often we make it difficult for people to avoid arguing with us, even though we protest to the end that we are the injured party. R. D. Laing is a professional psychiatrist who has studied the sources of human behaviour. 'I'm upset, you are upset' comes from a little book of imaginary exchanges called *Knots*.

William Blake had never heard of psychiatry, because it hadn't been invented when he was writing two hundred years or so ago. But very few people have had more piercing insights into human motivation than Blake. In 'A Poison Tree' he shows that it is not anger but malice that causes the real harm. You can be angry with anyone, even yourself. But with a friend you express your anger and then make up. It's the malicious storing of anger, so that it turns into hatred, that kills:

> I was angry with my friend:
> I told my wrath, my wrath did end.
> I was angry with my foe:
> I told it not, my wrath did grow.

How do you treat your friends? Friends can be one of the most important aspects of our lives, but they don't always get the treatment they deserve. They certainly get a rough ride in 'She Had More Friends' by Joanne Burns, and with Colin West's 'Frank' we're moving into the area of black humour. And that's where we stay, with Roger McGough's 'The Lesson':

> 'Please may I leave the room sir?'
> a trembling vandal enquired
> 'Of course you may' said teacher
> put the gun to his temple and fired

'The Lesson' is quite a favourite with teachers, though of course none of them would ever be tempted to run amok like that in your school – would they?

With John Agard's 'The Soldiers Came' we're confronted with the ultimate conflict – war. The First World War (1914–18) was fought 'to end all wars', but since then there have been a great many more, claiming millions of lives. It is a depressing thought that since 1945, when the Second World War ended, there has been some sort of armed conflict every year, right down to the Gulf War in 1991. Some wars last years, some are over in a few weeks. But however long they last, and whatever the result, they always inflict terrible sufferings on civilian populations caught up in the fighting. John Agard's poem acknowledges this, but puts in a bid for hope, hope in the future generation:

> Now the children
> are planting seedlings
> to help the forest grow again.

Of course, most conflict isn't on this sort of scale, and a lot of it happens in the home. Who does the washing up in your house? Why is the pedal-bin always full, and whose turn is it to empty it? Having to do things we don't want to do is a constant source of conflict. And having to do things we don't want to do with people we're always likely to clash with is even more dangerous as Michael Rosen's 'Washing Up' demonstrates.

Though conflict in real life needs to be taken seriously, it has always produced good comic material, and to say you shouldn't make jokes about it would be to ban a great deal of laughter. We can all enjoy the 'Adventures of Isabel' (Ogden Nash) and 'Algernon the Viking' (Terry Jones), though we know perfectly well that it's wrong to eat bears, punch doctors, or invade other people's territories. Perhaps the next time you feel a quarrel coming on, you could turn it into a poem instead.

I'M UPSET, YOU ARE UPSET

JILL   I'm upset you are upset

JACK   I'm not upset

JILL   I'm upset that you're not upset that I'm upset
you're upset

JACK   I'm upset that you're upset that I'm not upset
that
you're upset that I'm upset, when I'm not.

R. D. Laing

A POISON TREE

I was angry with my friend:
I told my wrath, my wrath did end.
I was angry with my foe:
I told it not, my wrath did grow.

And I watered it in fears,
Night and morning with my tears;
And I sunned it with smiles,
And with soft deceitful wiles.

And it grew both day and night,
Till it bore an apple bright;
And my foe beheld it shine,
And he knew that it was mine,

And into my garden stole
When the night had veiled the pole:
In the morning glad I see
My foe outstretched beneath the tree.

William Blake

SHE HAD MORE FRIENDS

she had more friends
than you could fit
into the back of a truck

that's why she didn't mind
leaving them parked
on a cliff edge

while she went
for a stroll
with the brake in her pocket

Joanne Burns

FRANK

We don't mention Frank
In this house any more;
No, not since he nailed
Mother's boots to the floor.
What makes matters worse
With regard to this crime
Is Mother was wearing
Her boots at the time.

Colin West

THE REBEL

When everybody has short hair,
The rebel lets his hair grow long.

When everybody has long hair,
The rebel cuts his hair short.

When everybody talks during the lesson,
The rebel doesn't say a word.

When nobody talks during the lesson,
The rebel creates a disturbance.

When everybody wears a uniform,
The rebel dresses in fantastic clothes.

When everybody wears fantastic clothes,
The rebel dresses soberly.

In the company of dog lovers,
The rebel expresses a preference for cats.

In the company of cat lovers,
The rebel puts in a good word for dogs.

When everybody is praising the sun,
The rebel remarks on the need for rain.

When everybody is greeting the rain,
The rebel regrets the absence of sun.

When everybody goes to the meeting,
The rebel stays at home and reads a book.

When everybody stays at home and reads a book,
The rebel goes to the meeting.

When everybody says, Yes please,
The rebel says, No thank you.

When everybody says, No thank you,
The rebel says, Yes please.

It is very good that we have rebels.
You may not find it very good to be one.

D. J. Enright

THE LESSON

A poem that raises the question:
Should there be capital punishment in schools?

Chaos ruled OK in the classroom
as bravely the teacher walked in
the hooligans ignored him
his voice was lost in the din

'The theme for today is violence
and homework will be set
I'm going to teach you a lesson
one that you'll never forget'

He picked on a boy who was shouting
and throttled him then and there
then garrotted the girl behind him
(the one with grotty hair)

Then sword in hand he hacked his way
between the chattering rows
'First come, first severed' he declared
'fingers, feet, or toes'

He threw the sword at a latecomer
it struck with deadly aim
then pulling out a shotgun
he continued with his game

The first blast cleared the backrow
(where those who skive hang out)
they collapsed like rubber dinghies
when the plug's pulled out

'Please may I leave the room sir?'
a trembling vandal enquired
'Of course you may' said teacher
put the gun to his temple and fired

The Head popped a head round the doorway
to see why a din was being made
nodded understandingly
then tossed in a grenade

And when the ammo was well spent
with blood on every chair
Silence shuffled forward
with its hands up in the air

The teacher surveyed the carnage
the dying and the dead
He waggled a finger severely
'Now let that be a lesson' he said

Roger McGough

THE SOLDIERS CAME

The soldiers came
and dropped their bombs.
The soldiers didn't take long
to bring the forest down.

With the forest gone
the birds are gone.
With the birds gone
who will sing their song?

But the soldiers forgot
to take the forest
out of the people's hearts.
The soldiers forgot
to take the birds
out of the people's dreams.
And in the people's dreams
the birds still sing their song.

Now the children
are planting seedlings
to help the forest grow again.
They eat a simple meal of soft rice
wrapped in banana leaf.
And the land welcomes their smiling
like a shower of rain.

John Agard

WASHING UP

On Sundays,
my mum and dad said,
'Right, we've cooked the dinner,
you two can wash it up,'
and then they went off to the front room.

So then we began.
First there was the row about who
was to wash and who was to dry.
My brother said, 'You're too slow at washing,
I have to hang about waiting for you,'
so I said,
'You always wash, it's not fair.'

'Hard cheese,' he says,
'I'm doing it.'
So that was that.

'Whoever dries has to stack the dishes,'
he says,
so that's me stacking the dishes
while he's getting the water ready.

Now,
quite often we used to have mustard
with our Sunday dinner
and we didn't have it out of a tube,
one of us used to make it with the powder
in an eggcup
and there was nearly always
some left over.

Anyway,
my brother
he'd be washing up by now
and he's standing there at the sink
his hands in the water,
I'm drying up,
and suddenly he goes,
'Quick, quick quick
come over here
quick, you'll miss it
quick, you'll miss it.'
'What?' I say, 'What?'
'Quick, quick. In here,
in the water.'
I say,

'What? What?'
'Give us your hand,' he says
and he grabs my hand
then my finger,
'What?' I say,
'That,' he says,
and he pulls my finger under the water
and stuffs it into the eggcup
with left-over blobs of old mustard
stuck to the bottom.
It's all slimey.
'Oh Horrible.'

I was an idiot to have believed him.
So I go on drying up.

Suddenly
I feel a little speck of water on my neck.
I look up at the ceiling.
Where'd that come from?

I look at my brother
he's grinning all over his big face.

'Oy, cut that out,'
He grins again
sticks his finger under the water
in the bowl and
flicks.

Plip.
'Oy, that got me right on my face.'
'Did it? did it? did it?'
He's well pleased.

So now it's my turn
I've got the drying up cloth, haven't I?
And I've been practising for ages
on the kitchen door handle.
Now he's got his back to me
washing up
and
out goes the cloth, like a whip, it goes
right on the –
'Ow – that hurt. I didn't hurt *you*.'
Now it's me grinning.

So he goes,
'All right, let's call it quits.'
'OK,' I say, 'one-all. Fairy squarey.'

So I go on drying up.
What I don't know is that
he's got the Fairy Liquid bottle under the
water
boop boop boop boop boop boop
it's filling up
with dirty soapy water
and next thing it's out of the water
and he's gone squeeesh
and squirted it right in my face.

'Got you in the mush,' he goes.

'Right, that's it,' I say,
'I've had enough.'
And I go upstairs and get
this old bicycle cape I've got,
one of those capes you can wear
when you ride a bicycle in the rain.

So I come down in that
and I say,
'Ok I'm ready for anything you've got now.
You can't get me now, can you?'

So next thing he's got the little
washing-up brush
and it's got little bits of meat fat
and squashed peas stuck in it
and he's come up to me
and he's in, up, under the cape with it
working it round and round
under my jumper, and under my chin.

So that makes me really wild
and I make a grab for anything that'll
hold water; dip it in the sink
and fling it at him.

What I don't know is that
while I went upstairs to get the cape
he's got a secret weapon ready.

It's his bicycle pump,
he's loaded it with the dirty washing-up water
by sucking it all in.
He picks it up,
and it's squirt again.
All over my hair.

Suddenly the door opens.
'Have you finished the . . .?'
It's Mum AND Dad.

'Just look at this.
Look at the pair of them.'

And there's water all over the floor
all over the table
and all we've washed up is
two plates and the mustard pot.

My dad says,
'You can't be trusted to do anything you're asked,
can you.'

He always says that.

Mind you, the floor was pretty clean
after we had mopped it all up.

Michael Rosen

A FABLE

A crazy hunter, following a bear,
And pressing harder than a man should dare,
Was menaced by a leopard and a lion.
Availed no prayer, no cries to Heaven or Zion,
For he had slain their cubs, and with vile blows,
And welded Sky to Jungle by their woes.

Gazing upon a tree, he swiftly fled.
But in his path the bear with turning tread
Firm hindered the supposed security.
Oh, what to do? How save himself from three?
Dropping his gun, he howled and beat the air;
Then, stretching wide his arms, embraced the bear.
'Save me, sweet beast!' he cried. 'Love! Lick my face!'
Which the bear did, returning the embrace.

You know the rest, you know that tightening squeeze.
Only to think, it makes your spirit freeze;
Only to think, it pulls you to the ground,
And makes your blood run cold, your head go round.

Moral: To wicked beasts be straight and fair;
But do not pet them. Face them, and beware!
And never drop your gun to hug a bear.

Herbert Palmer

ADVENTURES OF ISABEL

Isabel met an enormous bear;
Isabel, Isabel, didn't care.
The bear was hungry, the bear was ravenous,
The bear's big mouth was cruel and cavernous.

The bear said, Isabel, glad to meet you,
How do, Isabel, now I'll eat you!
Isabel, Isabel, didn't worry,
Isabel didn't scream or scurry.
She washed her hands and she straightened her hair up,
Then Isabel quietly ate the bear up.

Once on a night as black as pitch
Isabel met a wicked old witch.
The witch's face was cross and wrinkled,
The witch's gums with teeth were sprinkled.
Ho, ho, Isabel! the old witch crowed,
I'll turn you into an ugly toad!
Isabel, Isabel, didn't worry,
Isabel didn't scream or scurry.
She showed no rage and she showed no rancour,
But she turned the witch into milk and drank her.

Isabel met a hideous giant,
Isabel continued self-reliant.
The giant was hairy, the giant was horrid,
He had one eye in the middle of his forehead.
Good morning, Isabel, the giant said,
I'll grind your bones to make my bread.
Isabel, Isabel, didn't worry,
Isabel didn't scream or scurry.
She nibbled the zwieback that she always fed off,
And when it was gone, she cut the giant's head off.

Isabel met a troublesome doctor,
He punched and he poked till he really shocked her.
The doctor's talk was of coughs and chills
And the doctor's satchel bulged with pills.
The doctor said unto Isabel,
Swallow this, it will make you well.
Isabel, Isabel, didn't worry,
Isabel didn't scream or scurry.
She took those pills from the pill-concocter,
And Isabel calmly cured the doctor.

Ogden Nash

ALGERNON THE VIKING

Algernon the Viking
Had a funny sort of nose,
The sort that grows and grows
And grows and grows and grows.

When he was just a youngster,
Learning crime and doing wrong,
His olfactory organ
Was already two feet long.

His Mother said: 'It's lovely!'
But his Dad said: 'He's a freak.
I'll go and steal another
Child with a more standard beak.'

But his Mother wouldn't lose him,
And she gave him lots to eat,
So that by the time he'd reached
Six foot – his nose had reached his feet!

The girls all sniggered at him,
Called him 'Nosey Algernon',
And all he could reply was:
'Pnease! Nind what nyou're stnanding on!'

Then his Father built a warship
Saying: 'Let's go raiding, Chums!
Although guess who isn't in
The crew – no matter who else comes?'

Algy pleaded with his
Dad, but the reply was: 'No!
A conk like that is just
A drag – especially when we row.'

'No, it's lovely!' said his Mum,
'And if he lies flat on his back,
You can use his snozzle as
The mast – now go and help him pack.'

So the ship set off plus Algy
With the sail fixed to his nose
– A-turning and a-twisting
Catching every wind that blows.

And they'd never sailed so surely,
And they'd never sailed so fast,
As when Algernon the Viking's nose
Was turned into the mast.

Then they landed somewhere foreign,
Algy's Dad said: 'You stay here.
I'll not have our victims laugh
At us – they're meant to scream with fear.'

'Nonsense!' said his Mother
(Who enjoyed a trip at sea)
'You let him go and fight
With you, while I prepare the tea.'

So the Vikings leapt out screaming,
Curdling blood and frightening foes,
And Algy boldly followed with
His extraordinary nose.

And though he was behind
The rest, his nose stuck out ahead,
Complete with hairs and pimples
Yellow, pink and puce and red.

And Algy fought behind it
(Though he'd got a nasty cough)
And he chose to fight the fiercest
Foes – so they could cut it off.

But the enemy was stricken
When they saw that mighty trunk,
And they cried: 'St. Patrick save us!'
And did History's quickest bunk.

But just as one was running,
He returned with cut and thrust,
And he sliced right through young Algy's
Nose, and it fell down in the dust.

Algy toppled backwards,
For his balance was put out,
And he fell into a swoon
Now disencumbered of his snout.

Well the Vikings were victorious,
And they held a Victory Tea,
But Algy's Mum was shattered
When she saw her son nose-free.

Oh, Algy! It were lovely!
Your proboscis was my joy,
And now,' she cried, '*look* at you!
You're just like *any other boy*!'

And his Dad was really livid.
He began to rant and rail.
'You stupid little blighter!
Now we haven't got a sail!'

And so they had to row
Back home, leaving Algy there,
Feeling glad he'd lost his hooter,
But that Life was not quite fair.

Terry Jones

NIGHT AND DARK

Do you get spooked at night? Are you afraid of the dark? The night can be frightening – that inky blackness that cloaks everything, a long, poorly-lit lane you have to walk down, a strange house where you can't find the light-switches. Poets are just as likely to be scared of the dark as the rest of us; and as keen to make a lark out of it too – as Spike Milligan does in 'Bump!':

> Things that go 'bump!' in the night,
> Should not really give one a fright.
> It's the hole in each ear
> That lets in the fear,
> That, and the absence of light!

But however much we try to fool ourselves into making a joke of our fear, fear can be very real. Dorothy Livesay asks in 'And Even Now', 'Who was it that touched me? – What thing laughed?' Walter de la Mare is one of the greatest poets for atmosphere and his poem 'The Listeners' genuinely gives me the creeps.

In another marvellous poem, Dylan Thomas's 'Do Not Go Gentle Into That Good Night', the night equals death. The poem is addressed to Dylan Thomas's father and, although it accepts his death as inevitable, it is a tremendous rallying cry to the human spirit:

> Do not go gentle into that good night,
> Old age should burn and rave at close of day;
> Rage, rage against the dying of the light.
>
> Though wise men at their end know dark is right,
> Because their words had forked no lightning they
> Do not go gentle into that good night.

But night and dark are not always to be seen as hostile. 'Auld Daddy Darkness' by James Ferguson shows the comforting side of darkness, and no one would under-estimate the value of sleep – sleep, as Shakespeare puts it:

> that knits up the ravelled sleave of care,
> The death of each day's life, sore labour's bath,
> Balm of hurt minds, great nature's second course,
> Chief nourisher in life's feast . . .

You may think that's overdoing it, but the speaker, Macbeth, has just murdered his king. He knows his guilty conscience will prevent him from sleeping.

Most of us, fortunately, don't have dreadful crimes on our minds when we go to bed. A. A. Milne captures perfectly the experience of going to sleep in his poem 'In the Dark'. And, of course, once we're asleep, there's another whole world that comes very much to life. Judith Nicholls catches something of this nocturnal life in her poem 'Night'. If you ever go camping, or just stay up late on a beautiful, clear night, you too can join this world as a sort of spectator:

> where the night owl cries;
> where clambering roots
> catch at my feet
> where fox and bat
> and badger meet
> and night has eyes.

But finally as Eleanor Farjeon recognises in 'The Night Will Never Stay', the dawn will come as the earth turns on its axis, and the daytime world will yawn into life once more:

> The night will slip away
> Like sorrow or a tune.

NIGHT COMES

Night comes
leaking
out of the sky.

Stars come
peeking.

Moon comes
sneaking
silvery-sly.

Who is
shaking,
shivery,
quaking?

Who is afraid
of the night?

Not I.

Beatrice Schenk de Regniers

IN THE DARK

I've had my supper,
  And had my supper,
    And HAD my supper and all;
I've heard the story
  Of Cinderella,
    And how she went to the ball;
I've cleaned my teeth,
  And I've said my prayers,
    And I've cleaned and said them right;
And they've all of them been
  And kissed me lots,
    They've all of them said, 'Good-night.'

So – here I am in the dark alone,
   There's nobody here to see;
      I think to myself,
      I play to myself,
   And nobody knows what I say to myself;
Here I am in the dark alone.
   What is it going to be?
I can think whatever I like to think,
I can play whatever I like to play,
I can laugh whatever I like to laugh,
   There's nobody here but me.

I'm talking to a rabbit . . .
   I'm talking to the sun . . .
I think I am a hundred –
   I'm one.
I'm lying in a forest . . .
   I'm lying in a cave . . .
I'm talking to a Dragon . . .
   I'm BRAVE.
I'm lying on my left side . . .
   I'm lying on my right . . .
I'll play a lot to-morrow . . .
      . . . .
I'll think a lot to-morrow . . .
      . . . .
I'll laugh . . .
   a lot . . .
      to-morrow . . .
   (Heigh-ho!)
      Good-night.

A. A. Milne

AULD DADDY DARKNESS

Auld Daddy Darkness creeps frae his hole,
Black as a blackamoor, blin' as a mole;
Stir the fire till it lowes, let the bairnie sit,
Auld Daddy Darkness is no' wantit yet.

See him in the corners hidin' frae the licht,
See him at the window gloomin' at the nicht;
Turn up the gas licht, close the shutters a',
An' Auld Daddy Darkness will flee far awa'.

Awa' to hide the birdie within its cosy nest,
Awa' to hap the wee flooers on their mither's breast,
Awa' to loosen Gaffer Toil frae his daily ca',
For Auld Daddy Darkness is kindly to a'.

He comes when we're weary to wean's frae oor waes,
He comes when the bairnies are gettin' aff their claes,
To cover them sae cosy, an' bring bonnie dreams,
So Auld Daddy Darkness is better than he seems.

Shut yer een, my wee tot, ye'll see Daddy then;
He's in below the bed claes, to cuddle ye he's fain.
Noo nestle in his bosie, sleep an' dream yer fill,
Till Wee Davie Daylicht comes keekin' owre the hill.

James Ferguson

DO NOT GO GENTLE INTO THAT GOOD NIGHT

Do not go gentle into that good night,
Old age should burn and rave at close of day;
Rage, rage against the dying of the light.

Though wise men at their end know dark is right,
Because their words had forked no lightning they
Do not go gentle into that good night.

Good men, the last wave by, crying how bright
Their frail deeds might have danced in a green bay
Rage, rage against the dying of the light.

Wild men who caught and sang the sun in flight,
And learn, too late, they grieved it on its way,
Do not go gentle into that good night.

Grave men, near death, who see with blinding sigh
Blind eyes could glaze like meteors and be gay,
Rage, rage against the dying of the light.

And you, my father, there on the sad height,
Curse, bless, me now with your fierce tears, I pray.
Do not go gentle into that good night.
Rage, rage against the dying of the light.

Dylan Thomas

TEMPER

'Blow out the light,' they said, they said
   (She'd got to the very last page);
'Blow out the light,' they said, they said,
'It's dreadfully wicked to read in bed';
Her eyes grew black and her face grew red
   And she blew in a terrible rage.

She put out the moon, she did, she did,
   So frightfully hard she blew,
She put out the moon, she did, she did;
Over the sky the darkness slid,
The stars all scuttled away and hid –
   (A very wise thing to do).

But please don't whisper the tale about,
   She'd get into trouble, she would;
Please don't whisper the tale about,
If anyone else should ever find out
She'd get into trouble without a doubt,
   And now she's *ever* so good.

                   Rose Fyleman

IT'S DARK IN HERE

I am writing these lines
From inside a lion,
And it's rather dark in here.
So please excuse the handwriting
Which may not be too clear.
But this afternoon by the lion's cage
I'm afraid I got too near.
And I'm writing these lines
From inside a lion,
And it's rather dark in here.

Shel Silverstein

CAT IN THE DARK

Look at that!
Look at that!

But when you look
there's no cat.

Without a purr
just a flash of fur
and gone
like a ghost.

The most
you see
are two tiny
green traffic lights
staring at the night.

John Agard

NIGHT

There's a dark, dark wood
inside my head
where the night owl cries;
where clambering roots
catch at my feet
where fox and bat
and badger meet
and night has eyes.

There's a dark, dark wood
inside my head
of oak and ash and pine;
where the clammy grasp
of a beaded web
can raise the hairs
on a wanderer's head
as he stares alone
from his mossy bed
and feels
the chill of his spine.

There's a dark, dark wood
inside my head
where the spider weaves;
where the rook rests
and the pale owl nests,
where moonlit bracken
spikes the air
and the moss is covered,
layer upon layer,
by a thousand fallen leaves.

Judith Nicholls

THE LISTENERS

'Is there anybody there?' said the Traveller,
    Knocking on the moonlit door;
And his horse in the silence champed the grasses
    Of the forest's ferny floor:
And a bird flew up out of the turret,
    Above the Traveller's head:
And he smote upon the door again a second time;
    'Is there anybody there?' he said.
But no one descended to the Traveller;
    No head from the leaf-fringed sill
Leaned over and looked into his grey eyes,
    Where he stood perplexed and still.
But only a host of phantom listeners
    That dwelt in the lone house then
Stood listening in the quiet of the moonlight
    To that voice from the world of men:
Stood thronging the faint moonbeams on the dark stair,
    That goes down to the empty hall,
Hearkening in an air stirred and shaken
    By the lonely Traveller's call.
And he felt in his heart their strangeness,
    Their stillness answering his cry,
While his horse moved, cropping the dark turf,
    'Neath the starred and leafy sky;
For he suddenly smote on the door, even
    Louder, and lifted his head: –
'Tell them I came, and no one answered,
    That I kept my word,' he said.
Never the least stir made the listeners,
    Though every word he spake
Fell echoing through the shadowiness of the still house
    From the one man left awake:
Ay, they heard his foot upon the stirrup,
    And the sound of iron on stone,
And how the silence surged softly backward,
    When the plunging hoofs were gone.

Walter de la Mare

BUMP!

Things that go 'bump!' in the night,
Should not really give one a fright.
It's the hole in each ear
That lets in the fear,
That, and the absence of light!

Spike Milligan

AND EVEN NOW

When I was a child,
Lying in bed on a summer evening,
The wind was a tall sweet woman
Standing beside my window.
She came whenever my mind was quiet.

But on other nights
I was tossed about in fear and agony
Because of goblins poking at the blind,
And fearful faces underneath my bed.
We played a horrible game of hide-and-seek
With Sleep the far-off, treacherous goal.

And even now, stumbling about in the dark,
I wonder, Who was it that touched me? –
What thing laughed?

Dorothy Livesay

THE MOON

The moon has a face like the clock in the hall;
She shines on thieves on the garden wall,
On streets and fields and harbour quays,
And birdies asleep in the forks of the trees.

The squalling cat and the squeaking mouse,
The howling dog by the door of the house,
The bat that lies in bed at noon,
All love to be out by the light of the moon.

But all of the things that belong to the day
Cuddle to sleep to be out of her way;
And flowers and children close their eyes
Till up in the morning the sun shall rise.

Robert Louis Stevenson

THE NIGHT WILL NEVER STAY

The night will never stay,
The night will still go by,
Though with a million stars
You pin it to the sky;
Though you bind it with the blowing wind
And buckle it with the moon,
The night will slip away
Like sorrow or a tune.

Eleanor Farjeon

INDEX OF POEMS

INDEX OF POETS

ACKNOWLEDGEMENTS

The compiler and publishers would like to thank the following for their kind permission to reproduce copyright material:

John Agard c/o Caroline Sheldon Literary Agency for 'The Soldiers Came' from *Laughter is an Egg* published by Kestrel/Puffin, 1990 and 'Cat in the Dark' from *I Din Do Nuttin* published by The Bodley Head, 1983; Moira Andrew for 'Raspberry Jam'; Alan Brownjohn for 'We Are Going to See the Rabbit' from his *Collected Poems* published by Hutchinson; Sheila Colman, Literary Executor of Lord Alfred Douglas for 'The Shark'; Wendy Cope for 'Score'; John Cotton for 'Through That Door'; Curtis Brown, London, on behalf of the Estate of Sir John Betjeman for 'Harvest Hymn'; Curtis Brown Ltd for 'Sweet Dreams' © Ogden Nash 1962 and 'Adventures of Isabel' © Ogden Nash 1936; Charles Causley for 'Tell Me, Tell Me, Sarah Jane' from his *Collected Poems* and 'Dan Dory' from *Jack the Treacle Eater* published by Macmillan; David Higham Associates Ltd and Dent for 'Do Not Go Gentle Into That Good Night' © Dylan Thomas; Peter Dixon for 'I'd Like to Be a Teabag' and 'Colour of My Dreams'; Peggy Dunstan for 'Butterfingers'; Richard Edwards for 'If I Were the Conductor', 'If I Were an Astronomer', 'If I Were an Explorer' and 'If Only I Could Drive a Train'; Faber and Faber Ltd for 'Macavity: the Mystery Cat' from *Old Possum's Book of Practical Cats* by T.S. Eliot; Faber and Faber Ltd for 'Night' from *Magic Mirror* by Judith Nicholls; Faber and Faber Ltd for 'Second Glance at a Jaguar' from *Wodwo* and 'Moon Music' from *Poetry in the Making* by Ted Hughes; U.A. Fanthorpe for 'Stanton Drew'; Eleanor Farjeon for 'The Night Will Never Stay', 'Jazz-Man' and 'Ned' from *Silver, Sand and Snow* published by Michael Joseph Ltd and *The Children's Bells* published by OUP; John Foster for 'Sand'; The Estate of Robert Frost for 'Stopping by Woods on a Snowy Evening' from *The Poetry of Robert Frost* edited by Edward Connery Lathem, published by Jonathan Cape; Barbara Giles for 'The Late Express'; Greenwillow Books, a division of William Morrow & Company Inc. for 'Spaghetti! Spaghetti! from *Rainy Rainy Saturday* © 1980 Jack Prelutsky; Hamish Hamilton Ltd for 'When I Dance' and 'Mek Drum Talk, Man' © James Berry from *When I Dance* by James Berry, 1988; Emily Hearne for 'Courage'; John Johnson Ltd for 'Sea Talk' and 'I Often Meet a Monster' by Max Fatchen; Terry Jones for 'Dancing in the Dust', 'Algernon the Viking' and 'The Whaler'; David King for 'I Hate Greens' as published in *A Picnic of Poetry* selected by Anne Harvey and published by Blackie and Son Ltd; R.D. Laing for 'I'm Upset, You Are Upset' from *Knots* published by Tavistock Publications; Norman MacCaig for 'Uncle Roderick' from *Collected Poems* published by Chatto & Windus; David McCord for 'Song of the Train'; James MacGibbon, Executor of the Estate of Stevie Smith for 'The Galloping Cat' from *The Collected Poems of Stevie Smith* published by Penguin; Wes Magee for 'Who?' and